Shouting From The Margins
An Anthology of Sermons about Love & Liberation

By Rev. Caroline A. Morrison

<u>Table of Contents</u>

Ordinary Time

Have Compassion on Yourself (September 28, 2024)
No Kings for Me! (November 3, 2024)
A Radical Kinda Love (November 10, 2025)

Have Compassion on Yourself

By: Reverend Caroline Morrison
Reading: Mark 7:24-30

Theme: Self-Care is Divine…You can't care for others without it.

For those of you who have never written a sermon before, allow me to give you a peek behind the scenes. When you write a sermon, after you figure out what the theme of this sermon is going to be and what the readings are going to be, you research the reading by pulling out commentaries and you read what other people have said about the readings. Sometimes it's incredibly helpful, and then, there are other times. This reading is one of those other times.

You see the reading today caused a lot of consternation among the theologians that I read when it came to Jesus actions and words. Typically, they fell into one of two camps. They fell into either, the woman convinced Jesus that he was wrong, or, Jesus was just testing the woman, and she answered correctly. In this reading Jesus seems very out of character. However, I've seen this in Jesus before. This was an example of the humanity of Jesus.

I'm sure that most of you are familiar with the teaching that Jesus was not just God, but, he was also human. It's a key part of the trinitarian view of God. He is "of one in being with the father." As the apostle's creed says. He was divine and human at the same time, and yet, we often spend an inordinate amount of time focused on the divinity of Jesus.

We don't spend much time on him being hangry, or sad, or angry, or tired, and yet it is just as important as him being God. In today's reading it is the humanity of Jesus that we see. And the Jesus we find in this reading feels uncomfortably familiar in that context.

While there was disagreement among the theologians about Jesus' motivation for his actions, there was a consensus that Jesus went to Tyre to get away. He went to Tyre because they were gentiles, it was far away from Galilee, and they were not very likely to know him there. He went there to finally get some time off. Some respite…relaxation…to be refreshed and rejuvenated.

At this point in Mark, Jesus had been going hard in his ministry. He had raised numerous people from the dead, he had healed the sick and walked on water and fed 5000 plus people, his cousin had been killed, and he had been kicked out of his hometown. He had been questioned relentlessly by the elders and teachers. He was living in the margins of society with the people in the margins of society and he was frankly exhausted.

He was burnt out and so Jesus went to Tyre for some self-care. And while he's there trying his best to just breathe and be alone, this woman finds him, begging him to heal her child.

Now, in this moment, Jesus is seen as rude, because frankly, Jesus is rude to her and his break in character has so many very confused. But their confusion is because they aren't seeing Jesus as human…they are viewing him from the pedestal that so many keep Jesus on.

But I do, and, I recognize what comes next because I've done it so many times. I have gotten burned out and overwhelmed and I was dismissive and rude to people that matter the most to me before I even had the chance to think. Those snappy, out of character moments are ones that take so much more than I'm sorry.

So, when I look at Jesus in this reading, when I look at him call this woman and her child dogs, I recognize this person. Jesus was trying to rest in a place, and he didn't expect to be noticed and this woman came out of nowhere and begged him, scripture says she begged him to cast the demon out of her daughter. And his response was "let the children be fed first for it's not fair to take the children's food and throw it to the dogs." In that moment, Jesus allowed his compassion fatigue to overshadow his grace and love.

But, Jesus isn't the only one dealing with exhaustion. He's not the only person in the story. Heck, He's not even the only caregiver. So, let's look at the mother

The woman in this story is a mother who was caring for her sick child. And while some theologians look at this woman and they say that her daughter was healed by her faith, I think they missed the mark slightly because to me it doesn't sound like this is a woman whose child is newly ill. This sounds like a woman so desperate for someone to heal her child that she begged Jesus…she dropped to the floor and begged Jesus…to heal her child.

This sounds like a woman who has tried homeopathic means, and she has tried to see healers and doctors, but nothing has worked so far and she is willing to try anything at this point. So she hears that this man that has done all of this healing in Galilee is in town and she goes to him…and Jesus' compassion fatigue met her exhaustion. And we see a battle of the filterless.

She was exhausted to the point that when Jesus referred to her and her daughter as dogs and said the children needed to eat first before it would be time for the gentiles...when Jesus told her wait your turn it's not your time, she said "even the dogs get the scraps." She didn't argue her place as a gentile with him, she didn't argue her place as a woman, she didn't argue her place at all. She didn't participate in, what has come to be known as, the oppression olympics. She very simply and succinctly used his metaphor to show the flaw in his statement.

"Because of what you have said your daughter is healed." Theologians say this shows her faith healed her daughter, but honestly, it's so much deeper than that.

What we see here is very simply two exhausted people at the intersection of care. We find two oppressed people, with one begging the other to use the privilege he does have to help her.

Now, if I'm being completely honest with you I had very little idea where I was supposed to go with this sermon today. I got excited because it was the Syrophoenician woman. I got excited because this is one of those tales of a person speaking up to someone in power. And so I assumed that that was the direction the spirit was leading me to preach this morning. At one point this turned into a lecture on intersectionality.

Thank goodness I turned from there. Because yes, this is about speaking truth to power. The woman recognizes that Jesus has power, and she holds him accountable. But that isn't even the biggest part of this story because we have seen Jesus held into account by those less privileged before in other gospels. We've seen the woman at the well for example.

But in a modern context, when we read this, we see two exhausted people and what becomes of compassion when we find ourselves drained and empty. We live in a time were those on the margins are blamed for the struggles by the people in power. We live in a time where to simply survive we are expected to give our life to our jobs. We're expected to give our essence…our all…to give 110%...to quote the character Deadpool, to give "maximum effort" when it comes to our jobs, and whatever's leftover can be put into our passions and our families and our friendships.

And what we see in the reading today…that's what happens when that is our reality. Jesus, the Son of God, God themself, a person for whom compassion and love and grace are the key principles in their being, speaks not out of love on the margins, but, out of exhaustion.

I ended last year with around 90 hours of unused vacation time…and I'm a hospice chaplain. In the job I had before this, I had almost a month of unused vacation days. And that was human resources. I have a horrible self-care practice and that doesn't show in my work, it shows at home. It shows in the number of times that I have been dismissive and rude to my family. It shows in the times that I haven't been attentive to my friends. It shows when I'm in the car going from place to place. Because that exhaustion doesn't usually impact your job until you've run out of everything.

It hits me, honestly, that we have been told over and over that you're not supposed to let the battery on your phone get to 0% before you charge it. You're not supposed to let it completely empty. And for most of us, we listen to that rule of thumb. We treat our phones better than we do ourselves because we let ourselves get to empty before we decide we're supposed to recharge us.

So, in a time like today, when there is so much work to be done, when there is so much to speak against. There's so much to march for. When there are so many people who need your help; who need you to use whatever privilege you have to help, in a time when it seems that so many other people are pulling on you, we've got to start learning to practice self-care before we reach exhaustion. Because this story is completely different if Jesus wasn't exhausted already.

Most of us want desperately to be the mother in this situation. To be the one to speak truth to power. And we give all of our energy doing just that. We give all of our energy fighting for the rights we need and deserve. We give all of our energy doing our jobs. We give so much energy loving our neighbor that we have nothing left with which to love ourselves. And we return to rest and relaxation only after we reached the point of exhaustion.

My friends, if you take away nothing else from this these are the points: caring for others is draining. It was never going to be easy. Having compassion and grace all the time takes a lot out of you. So much so even God living among us in the person of Jesus was exhausted from caring for others all the time. So, make sure that you love yourself as you love your neighbors. That's right, it's a flippable command. Care for the person in the mirror and their needs as much as you care for the person outside the mirror and theirs.

That's honestly it. That's the whole point. That cliche that you can't love others till you love yourself is right. It requires most of us to unlearn what we have been taught is important. In the Methodist denomination John Wesley had a teaching when it came to money, "earn all that you can, save all that you can, and give all that you can." It broke down to earn what you need to be comfortable, save what you need to be comfortable in the future, and give everything else. So, I will end this like this, work hard enough that you can take time. Save enough of your energy so that you can enjoy that time of respite. And, everything else, that you have give to others.

No Kings for Me!

By: Reverend Caroline Morrison
Reading: Psalm 146 & 1 Samuel 8:6-14

Theme: Even in our failings, God remains faithful and waiting for us

The psalms are such an interesting group of writings. They are often attributed to King David. I know I have an image of a mix of David the shepherd, and David the king, when I think of the psalms but the fact of the matter is the psalms were written by a number of different authors over hundreds of years, and yes, David was one of them. But this particular one today, the author was anonymous and while we have no idea who it was that actually wrote it, we do have an idea of when this one was written. This is a Psalm of praise and was most likely written in the post exilic period of Israel which means it was written after the exile to Babylon when the Israelites had been freed and had started returning home.

It's important to know that timing so we can understand the psalmist's context. Because after the psalmist gives praise to God the first thing he says is, "Do not put your trust in princes, in mortals, in whom there is no help. When their breath departs, they return to the earth; on that very day their plans and policies perish." What a topical verse to deal with just a few days before an election right? It's almost like it was planned.

Why is that the first thing he leads off with? What are the Israelites trying to do now that they've been released from exile? Well, like most of us, if we've experienced a disaster, the first thing we try to do Is restore things to the way things were.

The psalmist here is making a plea to the people of Israel. You see the psalmist obviously knows scripture and knows the way things were when they were taken into exile is not the way God intended for things to be. We need only look back to 1st Samuel to see that. Before 1st Samuel there was no king.

The reason we have the book of Judges and the book of Ruth is because God appointed judges and prophets to ensure that things were being handled properly. But the last of the prophets in that line before the 1st king, was Samuel. And Samuel had gotten old, so he put his children in his place. The people didn't like his children and they didn't like being so different from the rest of the world that they knew, so the elders went to Samuel and they said, 'we want a king. We want a king just like everyone else.'

In 1st Samuel 8 we see the conversation that Samuel has with God about it:

> "7and the LORD said to Samuel, "Listen to the voice of the people in all that they say to you; for they have not rejected you, but they have rejected me from being king over them. 8Just as they have done to me, from the day I brought them up out of Egypt to this day, forsaking me and serving other gods, so also they are doing to you. 9Now then, listen to their voice; only—you shall solemnly warn them, and show them the ways of the king who shall reign over them." 18And in that day you will cry out because of your king, whom you have chosen for yourselves; but the LORD will not answer you in that day."19But the people refused to listen to the voice of Samuel; they said, "No! but we are determined to have a king over us, 20so that we also may be like other nations, and that our king may govern us and go out before us and fight our battles."

Their first king was Saul. And he was a great king until he wasn't. Then God anointed the next King, David was a man after God's own heart until that whole Bathsheba incident where he stayed home from the war, sent a man to his death to try and hide his indiscretions…you know the story. Because of that the next ones from his line just got worse and worse. Sure, Solomon was good and wise. But for hundreds of years, the kings turn people further and further from God. And ironically enough, it was the bad leadership of these kings in disregarding and leading people away from God that led the people to be exiled in the first place. The prophet Isaiah wrote a lot in the preexilic portion of the book about the Israelites, having no justice for the oppressed, and no care for the widow and the orphan, and that brought the judgment of God upon them.

But believe it or not we're not talking about the kings of Israel today we're talking about this psalmist in post-exilic Israel. So, the beginning of this Psalm he praises God the next part of this Psalm he says let's not go back to exactly how things were, let's set God as our king like we were supposed to in the first place and, he makes the case for why God is a better king than any person they could choose.

"Happy are those whose help is in the God of Jacob whose hope is in the Lord their God who made heaven and earth the sea and all that's in them." And he gave us a list of what a leader should be. And it's a list of traits that God already meets. Those traits are one who keeps faith forever. Who executes justice for the oppressed. Who gives food to the hungry. Who sets prisoners free. God opens the eyes of the blind. God lifts up those who are bowed down. God loves the righteous. God watches over the strangers. God upholds the widow and the orphan. And the way of the wicked, God brings to ruin.

As a people who claim that God sits at our head, that he is Lord over all, these are the traits we expect from God. In times of uncertainty as we live in today, we can expect these traits from God. There is no uncertainty in who God is. Now, some of them we probably can't expect from a representative that we choose to lead us and speak for us. I don't expect any candidate that is running to give sight to the blind for example. But, for me personally, I do expect someone that I vote for to ensure researchers have public funding to try to come up with ways that helped those whose eyesight is impaired to live normal lives.

Most of these standards within the list that the anonymous psalmist wrote are not impossible for a person to live up to. So, on this election weekend, as we prepare to go to our ballot boxes and cast ballots for people that we want to fill the leadership positions within this country and state, I would ask you if you've used this checklist when making your selections.

Is the person that you are selecting going to bear true faith and allegiance? Will that person execute justice for the oppressed? Will they give food to the hungry? Will they set prisoners free? Will they lift up those that are bowed down? Will they watch over the stranger and the immigrant? Will they uphold the orphan and the widow? And will they seek to not reward the way of the wicked?

The examples of God and Jesus should always be the gold standard up to whom we hold those looking to lead. Now, as clergy, I won't, and can't, tell you how to vote. I won't tell you for whom to cast your ballots, or what issues should be important to you as Christians. I leave that in the hands of Sophia, the spirit of God. I will, however, encourage you to vote. Let your voice and your choice be heard. And I ask if you will look for the standard of a desirable leader in the people for whom you vote?

A Radical Kind of Love

By: Reverend Caroline Morrison
Reading: John 13:31-35

Theme: When we look for God within each person, it becomes easier to love each person.

Across this country today pastors, rabbis, imams, and other religious leaders are stepping into pulpits and up to podiums to address congregations of divided people. Some of those people are mourning. Some of them are celebrating. All of them are anxiously waiting to see exactly what the future holds.

Many of us, myself included, have spent so much time in our own camps and communities where we felt safe that we stopped listening to those that were on the opposite side of us. The time or two that I did remember to listen, I found that underneath what was being said was the fact that both of us were scared. Some of our concerns were the same. But the places where we differed…they were places that neither one of us could very well see across.

So today, I join with religious leaders across the country in talking about healing. For me specifically, it's healing and remembering what makes me a Christian. It's healing through remembering what radical love looks like.

So, what exactly is radical love? What do I mean when I say radical love? The word radical is nowhere in the reading today. "I give you a new commandment, that you love one another. Just as I have loved you, you also should love one another. By this everyone will know that you are my disciples, if you have love for one another." The word radical is nowhere in there. But the idea that the love he was talking about in this reading is different than what is so often practiced, even to this day, that was radical.

Now if I'm being honest, which of course I am, I have heard this preached often as Jesus just talking to the group. This group of disciples gathered around him before he heads off to 'love one another as I have loved you' and I think we all know it's bigger than that. I think we all know that it was love one another with an asterix.

But luckily, we don't have to wonder what he meant because Jesus beautifully practiced what he preached. Jesus whole ministry was about radical love. When Jesus was asked 'who's my neighbor? You said love your neighbor, well, who is my neighbor?' Jesus chose for the parable a person that was the epitome of a pariah in Jewish life at the time. Jesus chose a Samaritan. We grew up hearing about the Good Samaritan but there's not the same stigma attached to it today. We don't feel it the same way, but, I bet you could pick a group out of the last election and put them in there and you would have exactly the same feeling. You'd run into the stigma.

See Jesus didn't have the hang ups that we so often do. Jesus is God after all. We know from Samuel during the choosing of David to be king, Samuel looks at all of the young men that have been gathered in this room he said surely the king that God wants is in this room and God says no, he's not.

> [7]But the LORD said to Samuel, "Do not look on his appearance or on the height of his stature, because I have rejected him; for the LORD does not see as mortals see; they look on the outward appearance, but the LORD looks on the heart."

So, God looks inward. Jesus looked inward. Jesus was able to look at the person and just see a person without all the political alliances and the different things that separate us. Jesus cared for everyone throughout the gospels Jew, Gentile, Roman. He had conversations with Samaritans, tax collectors he had dinner with, he just looked at the person.

But, Jesus knew that there are so many things that divide us that it distracts us sometimes from seeing the image of God in the other person, so, he clarified another answer to a question posed to him, “whatever you do to these the least you do unto me.” He said whenever you look at the margins you see me. I had a hospice patient once that told me he was worried that if Jesus showed up at his door, he wouldn't recognize him and my response to him was that according to Jesus, we were supposed to treat everyone as if they were Jesus. We shouldn't hold the best seat at the table for Jesus, we should just treat the person as if they're Jesus.

And there's that radical love. But that's that easy radical love because that's taking care of people that are in need. That's that easy radical love because I'm helping out someone that I recognize needs help. I see Jesus in the person that I can help. And it's easy for me to look on the margins and see Jesus there. It is easy for me to look at a homeless person and say hey, let me help you. What can I do to help you? In the back of our minds, we hear ‘I was naked, and you gave me clothes. I was hungry and you gave me food.’ Oh, this person's Jesus. It's easy to see Jesus among people that we recognize as being in need of something. It is harder for us to see Jesus in those we consider our enemies, opposition, oppressors…

Jesus says pray for your enemies because Jesus can't make anything easy. He says look, when you start taking care of yourself, and, you start taking care of everyone else umm pray for your enemies too. More specifically, Jesus says

43“You have heard that it was said, ‘You shall
love your neighbor and hate your enemy.’ 44But I
say to you, Love your enemies and pray for those
who persecute you, 45so that you may be children
of your Father in heaven; for he makes his sun rise
on the evil and on the good, and sends rain on the
righteous and on the unrighteous. 46For if you love
those who love you, what reward do you have? Do
not even the tax collectors do the same? 47And if
you greet only your brothers and sisters, what more
are you doing than others? Do not even the
Gentiles do the same?”

That radical love is getting a little heavier now, isn't it? Because Jesus isn't just saying here to love your enemy and pray for those who persecute you, (which is already something I think most of us are not practiced in) he humanizes our enemies. God makes the sunrise on the evil and on the good. God sends rain on the righteous and the unrighteous.

He is pulling some Ecclesiastes stuff out now. Everybody makes mistakes. Everybody has those days. Jesus is saying everyone experiences the hardships and everyone has felt this way at one point or another. And if you only stay with the people that lift you up, you never get higher than their hands can reach.

If you love those who love you, what reward do you have? What's the reward that comes from radical love? What's the reward that comes from taking care of your neighbor regardless of who they are, of loving your enemy and praying for those that persecute you? What is the reward Jesus is talking about? When we start seeing everyone as a child of God, when we start acting more like God and loving each person as if they're Jesus, when we start looking for the image of God in each person regardless of who they are or who they voted for, we start shaping this world to be more like heaven. We reveal a little bit more of the Kin-dom each time we practice radical love.

I can hear some of you thinking, “Caroline, Jesus may not have been adversarial necessarily, but he also wasn't passive.” And that's true. The one aspect of radical love I haven't talked about is flipping tables and holding people in power accountable for being hypocrites and broods of vipers. Because Jesus wasn't a pushover. He wasn't passive in his ministry.

When I say he practiced what he preached, sometimes he didn't preach it he just practiced it. And holding those that lead accountable for their actions and their teachings and the way that they're leading is a radical form of love. Because, if we look to the prophets in the Old Testament, what happened to the leaders that led people away from God? What happened to the leaders that led people to the point that there was no justice to be found for the oppressed? While the people were taken into exile the leaders were killed. They met their end.

So, in that, Radical love is a form of protest. It's a form of civil and social disobedience. It's civil disobedience because radical love calls us to protest. Radical love calls us to draw attention to things that are wrong in our society. Radical love calls us to vote. It calls us to write letters and speak at town halls. It calls us to show love for our leaders by holding them accountable to do the right thing and to lead down just paths. And practice social disobedience because we don't just look for Jesus in the margins and we don't just look for God in the faces of the marginalized. But, instead, we find the image of God in each person, and we look for Jesus everywhere.

So, to review, we are called to practice a radical form of love. We are called to introduce to this world a more radical form of love. It is how everyone knows that we are followers of Christ because we have a radical form of love for one another. And that radical form of love means that we treat others as we would Jesus. Regardless of who they are, regardless of what their need may be, and whether we can see their need or not, we treat them as we would Jesus. That radical form of love means that regardless of who the person is, regardless of if we can recognize the need in them, regardless of where they stand politically, and of what they've done to us and our community, we remember that each person is a holder of the image of God, and we look for it in them. Practicing that radical form of love means we get to see Jesus every day. It means we get to build in our head a more complete image of what God looks like because we're interacting with God in each person.

And it means helping to shape this world into one that is more just. It's helping our leaders to be more like God in the way that they lead. And that radical love says more to bring about the Kin-dom upon this earth than any sermon, and any prayer vigil ever will.

Advent

Waiting in Faith (December 1, 2024)
Schrödinger's Future (December 8, 2024)
Joy in the Present (December 15, 2024)
From Beginning to End: Sophia, our Wise, and constant, companion (December 22, 2024)

Waiting in Faith

By: Reverend Caroline Morrison

SCRIPTURE: Luke 1:5; 7-8; 11-20; 26-28; 30-35; 38 (NRSV)

Theme: Even in times of trial, faith for tomorrow can be found.

The entire purpose of advent is anticipation and preparation while we await the celebration of the birth of Jesus. And this Year, I feel like the preparation and waiting for things to happen is destroying me on the inside. This sermon may have been one of the hardest ones I've ever written because it forced me to figure out why this time of waiting hasn't been the excited anxiousness that I felt in the past. As I meditated on faith and the reading for this week, I found myself struggling. For better or for worse many of us are experiencing anxiety as we wait for January 20th. For many of us here this period of waiting and preparation and anticipation had been joined with dread and fear as we wait to find out exactly what the future holds.

And so, I prayed as I got ready for this sermon and I deleted page after page of attempts that just didn't seem to flow properly because I wasn't listening to what I was being told, I allowed my fear to write instead of allowing the spirit to write.

Have you ever done that? Have any of you ever allowed your fear to make the decisions for you? Then, as I re-read the reading for today, I couldn't help but marvel at the way Mary handled what she had just been told. You see for Elizabeth after she figured out, she was pregnant (because her muted husband couldn't tell her what was going on) she secluded herself for five months and then she came out of seclusion proclaiming, "this is what the Lord has done for me when he looked favorably And took away the disgrace I have endured among my people."

For Elizabeth, her pregnancy was seen as a blessing. It brought liberation and redemption. For Mary, an unwed virgin, engaged to a man named Joseph, this pregnancy she was being told about could easily see her cast out from her home and losing her betrothed. She stood to lose everything. And yet, her response to Gabriel was simple, "Here am I, the servant of the Lord; let it be with me according to your word."

Mary had to be the definition of anxious as she told her family and Joseph what had happened. What had been told to her. For Zechariah and Elizabeth, they at least had precedent on their side. Stories of the prophet Abraham and his wife Sarah also having a child later in life are still well known. But, for Mary...hers was new.

Now to be clear, the idea of God calling, and using, a systemically oppressed person wasn't new. The margins are usually where God seems to call from regardless of how white, male, and cishet various denominations might keep the ranks of the ordained. But, within scripture, I have found there are actually three types of prophetic call story. Prophetic Work, found in stories such as Noah and Joshua. Prophetic Word, found in stories such as Moses and Jeremiah. And, Prophetic Motherhood...found only in this story right here. Please don't misunderstand, I am not saying that Mothers don't work or speak prophetically, rather, those called to prophetic motherhood seem to have traits of both. I'm merely saying that this is the only call to prophetic motherhood we find in scripture.

Within Prophetic work, there is typically not an argument or scene where the called person questions God's call. They simply answer the call before them. With Prophetic Word, those called usually have a moment when they are shown giving God the reason's they are not the right person for the job. Moses stuttered, Jeremiah was just a child, and Mary...She was a virgin. Yet, they all received what I call the promise to the prophets...a promise that God will be with them. There is never a requirement that they change, just answer the call and God will be with you. For Mary, the angel says, "The Holy Spirit will come upon you, and the power of the Most High will overshadow you."

I also find it interesting looking at Zechariah's reaction to Gabriel versus Mary's. Zechariah's reaction according to verse 12 says that he was terrified, and fear overwhelmed him and so the Angel said do not be afraid Zechariah. For Mary, the Angel greeted her, and she was perplexed by his words and pondered what sort of greeting it might be. Gabriel said do not be afraid Mary, but I think that's because that's what he's supposed to say, and he wasn't necessarily prepared for a teenager to not be afraid.

So, Mary said, "here am I, the servant of the Lord; Let it be with me according to your word". She had faith that she would be taken care of. She had faith that she wouldn't be ostracized. And we know that because she didn't ask about Joseph. She didn't ask how he was going to react to the news. And if we jump over to the book of Matthew really quickly after he does his Genealogy of Jesus, we find Gabriel's conversation with Joseph.

In Matthew 1:19 it says her husband Joseph being a righteous man and unwilling to expose her to public disgrace, planned to dismiss her quietly. But just when he'd resolved to do this, an Angel of the Lord appeared to him in a dream. When Joseph awoke from sleep, he did as the Angel of the Lord commanded him and took her as his wife. So, her fear of being dismissed was very real. But even though she was undoubtedly anxious, that anxiety and fear didn't cause her to falter in her Faith.

It had me wondering about the origin of faith and what would make hers so much stronger than mine felt at the moment? I've heard it said that faith is the evidence of things unseen which is a rewording of what we find in the letter to the Hebrews, "faith is the assurance of things hoped for the conviction of things not seen." That letter also talks about a cloud of witnesses.

In other words, stories…testimonies of all of the times that God has done things here all of the things that are attributable to God. Upon that historical basis we can build our faith.

That's what Mary's faith was built on. The history of what God had done for her people. She was living under the oppression of Rome. She was living in a time when the patriarchy wasn't as intangible an oppressor. She was likely just as much the property of her father as she would be the property of her husband. But she knew the stories of her people all of the times that God had seen them through. And she lived with such great faith-based on that the Angel said she was favored by God.

So where does that leave us? As we sit in this advent time, this time of preparation and anticipation and waiting, how do we find faith like Mary? When our fears are so justified, how do we keep faith strong enough that it isn't overcome by our fears? Look around you. The faces that you see seated next to you, they don't just provide you encouragement. They don't just provide you with fellowship. Your siblings in Christ help remind you that even in those times of oppression and darkness, God continues to work. So many times, I can look back and see that God is bigger than my fears. If the prejudices of humanity cannot stop the call of God, then our fear cannot stop the work of God.

When my wife and I sat across from my district superintendent and came out to her I was afraid I would lose everything. We had in fact been warned do not do it unless we were prepared to lose everything. And we did lose a lot. We lost friends. I have family I haven't talked to in years. That was 2017.

In 2024, I still have my wife and my children. I graduated seminary and God opened a door for me to be ordained. I have a ministry setting that I love. I still get opportunities to preach now and then.

So, we can acknowledge the anxiety we have for the future. Jesus did. In the garden of Gethsemane Jesus asked God to take it away. If Jesus felt it, then fear and anxiety of the future is simply part of being human. The beautiful thing about it is that we know that God is waiting for us in the future while accompanying us in the present. God can be seen throughout our past.

Our faith in God need not be blind. It need not be built on the experiences of others. Our faith can be built in the ways that God has, is, and will work in our community and our lives. Oppressive regimes didn't stop Mary's faith, oppressive practices didn't stop her willingness to answer her call, and, they won't stop ours either. They won't stop our work, they won't stop our witness, and they won't stop our call, because the work of Love continues…and you can have faith in that.

Schrödinger's Future

By: Reverend Caroline Morrison
Reading: Luke 1:14-17, 32-33 (NRSV)

Theme: There can be no hope while living in Schrödinger's Future.

Before we get started, I want to take a moment and let you know that we are going to be discussing the traditional advent topic of quantum mechanics today. But, if you bear with me, I promise, It's relevant.

The year was 1932 and in Austria a middle-aged theoretical physicist had postulated an equation that provided a way to calculate the wave function of a system and how it changed dynamically over time. He called it “quantum entanglement.” A year later Erwin Schrödinger won a Nobel Prize for his contributions to quantum physics.

His equation began to be used as a way to show probabilities and possibilities of where particles could be found. This gave birth to what has become known as the Copenhagen interpretation which says a particle doesn’t have a definitive location until a measurement is made. Simply put, multiple things can be true at once until you look to see which is actually true.

So, in 1935, Erwin Schrödinger decided to put forth what's become known as Schrödinger's cat paradox. It's a theoretical physics thought experiment. Essentially you make a cat sleep and then you put that cat in a box and seal the box. Now in the box with the cat you put the little radioactive piece from a Geiger counter which over the course have one hour an atom may or may not decay. And if it does decay then a counter tube discharges and through a relay, it releases a hammer which shatters a small flask of hydrocyanic acid.

Finally, you leave it for an hour. Now during that hour since you don't know what's happening in the box, the cat may continue to be alive, or an atom might decay, which would lead to the cat's death. Ultimately, you won't know which is true until you open the box and observe. And so, in that instance the cat can be both alive and dead concurrently.

For those of us here this morning, We sit in the present looking at what I will call Schrödinger's Future paradox. From where we sit, the future can look dark…bleak…hopeless. But, in the tradition of the cat paradox, that also means that somehow the future can at the same time look bright, cheerful, and hopeful.

Frankly, it's just harder to see the brighter option sometimes. In times like these, it's easy to be hopeless. It's easy to be engulfed by helplessness, to allow ourselves to become victims to chaos that feels out of our control. To feel forgotten, abandoned, abused, and victimized. So, if we have difficulty finding hope in the future, maybe we should start our focus instead…on the past. Focus back and regain our bearings a bit.

The reading today, tells us who John and Jesus are going to be. Zachariah is told by the angel that John will be great in the sight of the Lord. He'll be filled with the Holy Spirit, turn many to God, he'll have the spirit and power of Elijah. He will turn the hearts of parents to their children and turn the disobedient to the wisdom of the righteous and he will make people prepared for the Lord. Knowing who John will be means so much hope. Invoking the memory of Elijah brings hope for power and strength and Justice. Elijah was one of the Major prophets and one of the only humans in scripture to have ascended to heaven before death. A flaming chariot came and picked him up…A heavenly uber. So, finding out that your child was going to have the spirit and power of Elijah?? That's overwhelming, but, hopeful.

When the angel appeared to Mary, he said that Jesus will be great. He'll be called "son of the most high." He'll sit on the throne of David. Why is that important? Why was it important to say that Jesus would sit on the throne of David? Our teachings tell us that Jesus isn't just the son of God, he is God, and as we learned at the beginning of November, God didn't want a king over their people. God wanted to be on the throne over the people. And so, if Jesus is sitting on the throne of David, then God is giving a way to satisfy both desires, a person on the throne who is also God.

And what hope does that bring? Well, if you remember from the reading in Samuel, we found a list of the leadership traits of God: eternal, creator, faithful, justice bringer, provider, liberator, healer, restorer, protector of the burdened, the widow, and the orphan. A leader was being given to us that could finally have all of the traits no other human could.

And you know this isn't just beautiful for us as Christians. For our Muslim siblings the coming of these two men, whom they view as prophets, also brought Hope. According to the Quran in the 19th Surah called Mary, because they have an entire book named after Mary, the mother of Jesus, which, interestingly enough, is something we don't have in the Bible, John was given wisdom and tenderness by God. He would be devout. He would be kind to his parents and peace would be upon him his whole life.

Now the Koran does deviate some from our scripture some. For example, while the annunciation of Mary is in the Quran, the angel appears to Mary but it's not the angel that tells Mary who Jesus would be, instead it's Jesus. In verse 27 of the Surah it says that she came back to her people carrying the child and they said Mary you have done something terrible sister of Aaron! Your father was not a bad man; Your mother was not unchaste! She pointed at him. They said, "how can we converse with an infant?" but he said: 'I am a servant of God. He has granted me the scripture; Made me a prophet; Made me blessed wherever I may be. He commanded me to pray, to give alms as long as I live, to cherish my mother. He did not make me domineering or graceless. Peace was on me the day I was born and will be on me the day I die and to the day I am raised to life again." such was Jesus, son of Mary.

You see, the story is maybe more than a little different, but, regardless of where you read it, Jesus' birth was about hope. In a time when religious leaders and political leaders were corrupting influences on the population once again, the announcement of Jesus birth brought hope among his people. We'll see that on Christmas. And we can hear it in the Christmas carols that have been playing for months now.

Jesus birth still brings hope, but more importantly we know that there's more to the story. We know that Jesus wasn't just born in a manger, and that's all. Our hope stems from the fact that we know the tomb was empty. Our hope stems from knowing Jesus ascended into heaven. Our hope stems from knowing that Jesus continues to walk among us. It reminds me of the Easter hymn, He lives! He lives! Christ Jesus lives today! He walks with me and talks with me along life's narrow way! He lives! He lives! Salvation to impart! You ask me how I know he lives? He lives within my heart! He lives in each of us and where two or more are gathered in his name...he is there as well. Because for us, the story of Jesus isn't just a story about the past, it's about the present, and the future.

In times like this where things seem hopeless, we have all the ingredients we need to make a hopeless future. We always do. We have all the things we need to swing the pendulum to the dark side of the paradox. Like I said at the beginning of this it's easier to be hopeless because hopelessness requires you to do nothing. Hopelessness requires you to wallow. It requires you to feel depressed. Hopelessness requires helplessness. To be hopeless you need to feel powerless and resigned. And wow...I have been there. I still visit sometimes. Because sometimes it's impossible not to. Life hits you with setback after setback until you are on the ground thinking it would just be easier to stay down. The future we are facing seems daunting and destined to be horrible. And frankly, those feelings of powerlessness and hopelessness are valid.

But our hope for tomorrow stems from our faith in the promise of a God among us who continues to be here. Our hope lay in a future that is not set in stone. A future that is not written. Because just as we have all the ingredients for a hopeless future, we **ARE** the ingredients for a hopeful future. And just as the outcome of the Copenhagen interpretation is only set when observed, the future only becomes set when we decide to be still and do nothing.

You and I have each been called to serve God and one another. Though we may feel powerless before the shadows of future adversity, we are empowered by the creator of this universe to stand tall and declare we serve a God of justice, love, and peace. We serve a God who has already placed a path for a better future before us; a God who will walk with us on that path and meet us at the end. And with the never-ending hope in a living, loving God that is for us, with us, and in us, we will not be victims of a future that happens to us, we will be benefactors of a future we help to create.

Joy in the Present

by: Reverend Caroline Morrison
Reading: Luke 1:46-56

Theme: With strong anchors in Faith and Hope we can overcome conditioned fear and know the ***Joy and Peace*** God designed us to know.

On August 7, 1974, around dawn, renowned Frenchman Philippe Petit stepped out onto a 1-inch-thick cable suspended around 412 meters, or about 1/4 mile, above the ground. Over the course of about 45 minutes, he made eight passes between the towers of the World Trade Center walking, kneeling, laying down, saluting, just being in that moment. He described his walk between the towers as an act of artistic expression and personal fulfillment and he often spoke about the suspension, silence, and nothingness that he experienced while he was walking on the wire.

He got onto that wire with faith in his six years of experience and instruction, with the hope that he would be alive at the end of his walk, and that his artistic expression would make for a better world, and he found joy and peace while he was on the tightrope.

Within today's reading we find those same 3 elements. Today's reading is commonly referred to as the Magnificat. It's the song of Mary. It's one of the four songs of praise attributed to women in scripture. There's the song of Miriam found in exodus, the song of Deborah found in judges, the song of Hannah found in first Samuel, and today's reading the Magnificat found in Luke. In all of these songs of praise we find faith in the things God has done, hope for the things God will do, and joy for the things God is doing.

The song of Miriam is probably the simplest of the three. It is one sentence long. It has implied faith, implied hope, and expressed joy. “Sing to the Lord, for he has triumphed gloriously; horse and rider he has thrown into the sea.” It's also the only one of the four songs that actually has a rhyme scheme. But it's an example that your faith and your hope can be implied and your joy simply expressed.

Hannah's prayer begins with joy, much like Mary's does. In fact, her prayer and Mary's share very similar structures throughout. Faith, Joy, and Hope are all present but they're kind of jumbled around. And Deborah's song in the book of judges is honestly more like a one act play. Of the four, Deborah's really deserves its own sermon series. There is joy, faith, and hope for sure, but, there's also drama, and betrayal, murder, and liberation. It's an epic song and if you haven't read it, please go do it. Perhaps one of the times I come back next, we'll do a series about it. For now, just know that it also includes expressions of joy, faith, and hope.

For Mary's Magnificat, specifically, she pronounces her faith saying that God showed strength through his arms, scattered the proud in the thoughts of their hearts, brought down the powerful from their Thrones, lifted up the lowly, filled the hungry with good things, and sent the rich away empty. And God has kept his promises. Her hope is that all generations will call her blessed and God will show mercy to the people. And her joy is found in her soul magnifying the Lord, in her spirit rejoicing in God, and that God has done many great things for her and her people.

Now you might notice as you read the Magnificat that faith, joy, and hope, aren't necessarily neatly laid out in that order. And that's OK. They don't have to be. The point is that they are there. They're expressions of past, present, and future. They exist on a spectrum or a tightrope if you will. And just like Mr. Petit, you and I walk our own tightrope each day. Our faith behind us gives us strength, our hope before us giving us a reason, and peace and joy are with us each moment along the way.

Now I'm sure that there are those who recognize the idealized nature of this spectrum. Because, well, it is. Faith, joy, and hope are ideal. That's how our walk each moment should be. If our faith and our hope are strong, then our tightrope in between stays firm, and we stay balanced as we experience joy and peace.

But our reality is often much less like Phillipe's tightrope and more like Peter's stroll on the water in the Gospels. In the book of Matthew, after Jesus feeds the 5000 men plus the uncounted women and children, he tells the disciples to get into a boat and go to the other side of the sea while he dismisses the crowds. And then he went up to pray on a mountain. While he was praying, the boat was being battered by waves.

Early in the morning Jesus showed up strolling on the water toward the boat. The disciples cried out “it's a ghost” and Jesus said no it's not a ghost it's me don't be afraid. Peter said “Lord, if it's you command me to come to you on the water” and Jesus said “come.”

So, in doing that, Peter sets his anchor in faith in the things he's seen Jesus do, and hope that he'll be able to reach Jesus where he is at. And he steps out of the boat onto his tightrope. Scripture says that he starts walking on the water and going towards Jesus but when he noticed the strong wind he became frightened and began to sink. When his attention was no longer between that hope and his faith, his peace on the tightrope disappeared he became frightened.

He cried out to the Lord to save him, and Jesus reached out his hand and caught him and said, “you of little faith, why did you doubt?” It calls to mind another incident earlier in Matthew's gospel. The disciples are again on a boat in a storm, and they wake Jesus up pleading “Jesus save us. We're perishing.” and Jesus said, “why are you afraid, you of little faith?” And he calmed the storm.

Jesus inference that he finds his disciples lack of faith disturbing has always felt a little strange to me. And then I placed them on this line. The disciples and Peter showed no sign of peace or joy in either of these experiences. Both the disciples and Peter show fear and are referred to as having little faith. So, if we're maintaining the tightrope metaphor, fear exists when either faith or hope is lacking. Fear becomes a factor when one of our anchors starts to fail.

Because what we see through the example of Jesus in both of these experiences is when faith and hope continue to be strong anchors, then you have calm and peace. Fear exists outside the tightrope. Fear isn't a part of the natural order of things. If you look in Genesis, fear isn't mentioned until the apple is eaten. It's how God knows that something is wrong. God is walking through the garden, and he can't find Adam and Eve because they hid out of fear and embarrassment.

We were never meant to live in fear. I'll say that again. We weren't meant to have lives where we were afraid. We weren't designed to be afraid of God. That's why the first words out of the mouth of nearly every angelic encounter we find in scripture includes the words, do not be afraid, well, that and biblically accurate angels are really crazy! Jesus said it to the disciples as he walked up to the boat, "do not be afraid." I'm not one to ascribe a lot of theological accuracy to Monty Python, but, the scene where they encounter God in Monty Python and The Holy Grail and God tells them to stop groveling and to stop saying they aren't worthy, just be there in the moment and hear what God is saying. Honestly that's probably how God feels. We spend so much time telling God how unworthy we are we forget to actually listen to what God's telling us.

For many of us here, the first trauma we had to deconstruct was this belief that we were meant to fear God. I remember reading Sinners in the Hands of an Angry God in high school, and, I've heard more than my share of fire and brimstone sermons. I was taught that I was supposed to love God and fear God, and that God wanted a personal relationship with me. And I'm here to tell you that I have done quite a bit of study on relationships and if you fear your partner in the relationship then it is a toxic situation. You shouldn't live in fear of reprisal from the being you have a personal relationship with…from your very creator. Reverence isn't the same thing as fear. You can be reverent of God, and still not live in fear of God.

We were never meant to have a reason to be afraid Of God. In fact, the love of God for each one of us and the ability for each one of us to depend upon God is the reason we can have joy and peace between faith and hope. A life lived in fear, after all, is a life wasted. It's a life with no joy, with no peace. It's a dark and dreadful and chaotic life. It's a life God never intended us to have.

Our culture is such that fear is used as justification. It's seen as a necessary part of life. The Patriot Act exists because of fear. It was the main justification for the war in Iraq. McCarthyism was born out of fear. The red scare came out of fear. The internment of Japanese Americans during World War 2 came out of fear. That it took 35 years for gay men to not be banned for life from donating blood at all was a decision based in fear. And, just as Peter sank when he allowed fear to distract him and loosen his anchors of faith and hope, humanity makes its worst decisions when fear distracts us from the life of joy and peace God wants for us to have.

Living a life of joy and peace therefore requires us to have the courage to be countercultural. If a life of fear is a cultural expectation, then a life without it is courageous. Our longest serving president, Franklin Roosevelt, declared to the nation that courage isn't the absence of fear, but rather the assessment that something else is more important than fear. When you're courageous enough to not let fear stop you it's because you found something bigger than the fear you were supposed to feel. I would amend that quote to say that courage isn't the absence of fear, it is instead daring to find peace and joy in the face of it.

Lots of us are people pleasers, right? Ok, we've got at least one. Bringing joy to other people? That's an easy thing to do. Keeping any joy for ourselves, that's the hard thing.

The fact is that for better or for worse we are human. As strong as our faith and our hope may be, we will occasionally be distracted by the fear and uncertainty that exist around us. Oh, we can be cautious and realistic as we stand on our tightrope and balance. We can realize how fragile the joy and peace we're experiencing are. But, as much as some may like to believe themselves to be perfect, we really aren't. We have spiritual attention deficits…it's S.A.D. We are easily distracted, and we have issues with object permanence when it comes to our faith and hope.

And how do we fix that? Do we wear blinders? Do we close our eyes and plug our ears so we can be ignorant of everything outside our tight rope? Once I lose sight of my faith or my hope how do I get it back? How do I rebuild those broken anchors so that I feel secure enough to experience joy and peace again?

That's where the examples of the songs of praise come into this. Many of us are practiced in praying the words Christ taught us. Simply saying that phrase probably started the Lord's Prayer in some of your heads. Some of us are even practiced in praying in public. There are even some strange people who enjoy praying in public. But, most of us are not practiced in praising like our foremothers in scripture. While many of us have probably written out a wish list for the things we hope will happen in the future at some point in our life, I would venture to guess that most of us are not very well practiced in writing down the things God has done for us in our life.

Look, faith may be the evidence of things unseen, but, there is no reason we can't have evidence we can see of our faith. How can we expect our faith to be strong if we don't revisit why we have it in the first place? How can we expect to experience joy in the now, if we don't occasionally revisit the reasons why we should be feeling that joy and peace to begin with?

And so, I give to you, over the next week, a homework assignment. I'd like you to take your piece of paper here. Hold it up. So, take that piece of paper and fold it in half lengthwise. If you did it the short way, that's fine…just unfold it and fold it the long way. I think some of you probably see where I'm going with this. Over the next week I want you to occasionally take this out and I want you to build your anchors. Practice starting from one side and express the reasons for faith, then go to the other side and set your anchor for hope. And then, as we used to say when the yellow pages still existed, the fact that this is yellow is just a happy accident, let your fingers do the walking. As your fingers walk the line, meditate on the reasons you have for joy in that moment.

Use this as a tool to start building your song of praise. To practice identifying your anchors and experiencing your joy and peace. Set yourself on that line between your faith and hope and use the space to shout out your joys and know peace in those moments where you find silence. Because you don't just deserve to not be afraid, you deserve to be joyful in the knowledge that you are a beloved child of God. You deserve to know the peace of being wrapped in God's love. And you deserve to be practiced in finding the joy in the present and peace in each moment.

From Beginning to End: Sophia, our wise, and constant, companion

By: Reverend Caroline Morrison
Reading: Genesis 1:1-2 & John 14:26-27

Theme: Sophia=an expression of wisdom, creation, and love

"Whenever I get gloomy with the state of the world, I think about the arrivals gate at Heathrow Airport. General opinion started to make out that we live in a world of hatred and greed, but, I don't see that. Seems to me that love is everywhere. Often, it's not particularly dignified or newsworthy, but, it's always there. Fathers and sons, mothers and daughters, husbands and wives, boyfriends, girlfriends, old friends. When the planes hit the twin towers, as far as I know, none of the phone calls from the people on board were messages of hate or revenge; they were all messages of love. If you look for it, I have a sneaky feeling, you'll find that love, actually, is all around."

That is the opening monologue from the Christmas classic, Love, Actually, from 2003. Hugh Grant sounds much better saying the lines than I just did, that's for sure. Finding a movie about love this time of year is, perhaps, the easiest of all year. There are entire channels devoted to romantic comedies and romantic dramas. The hallmark movies have become the source of regular memes and humor with their often Christmas cookie cutter plots and characters. But, that is because there is a familiarity to them that brings comfort and a hope in the stories that things will work out and that stranger the protagonist met at the local cider mill that is being closed down by the corporation trying to buy the town might actually be a relative of Santa's.

Seriously, though, perhaps more than any other time of year, including valentine's day, and the commercialism of Christmas aside, Christmas seems to be focused on love. Of the hundreds of thousands of Christmas songs, it's estimated that tens of thousands have themes of some kind of love. Romantic, familial, or just goodwill and kindness are perhaps the most popular themes. Of those, there are hundreds of Christmas hymns…and I bet you can't guess what the regular theme of those hymns is. Power, and presents, of course! I'm just kidding, it's obviously love. I kind of have a theme going here after all.

Since it's often said that love came down at Christmas, let's take a second and familiarize ourselves with the cast of characters who make this season possible. We have Mary, Joseph, Gabriel, and Jesus. There are other more minor characters such as Zachariah and Elizabeth and shepherds and that inn keeper. But, in that first tale of advent, the first, and second readings of this sermon series…in the annunciation of Mary, there are only 4 characters mentioned. Gabriel, Mary, Jesus, and the oft unspoken heroine of the story…Sophia, the Holy Spirit. In fact, I would venture to say that the Holy Spirit is perhaps the most under-appreciated member of the trinity, let alone of the advent cast.

That the Holy Spirit is not seen as a "main character," particularly in comparison to the other two members of the Trinity, is not an idea based solely on conjecture. Rather, it's an idea based more out of observation. Take the apostles creed for example. Authorship for the creed is unknown; however, scholars have been able to determine that it was likely created around the 2nd century CE. And it is a very simplistic statement of faith. While it does not delve deep into the theology of who God is, it spends quite a bit on who Jesus is. And as for the Holy Spirit? The Apostles creed acknowledges that Jesus was conceived by the Holy Spirit. But our theology of the Holy Spirit in this is simply, I believe in the Holy Spirit. That's it. One sentence. Neither very informative, nor, inspiring.

The Nicene creed on the other hand was a product of the first council of Nicaea in 325 CE. This council was brought together specifically to cement a theological statement on the Trinity as well as develop a cannon. It was brought together as a way to speak back against several heresies that were being proclaimed. As it's designed to be a theological statement on the Trinity, we do have a little more on the spirit. It says, "I believe in the Holy Spirit, the Lord, the giver of life, who proceeds from the father and son who, with the father and the son is adored and glorified, who has spoken through the prophets." Those few sentence fragments aside, the spirit has been responsible for so much more. She was there and responsible for creation. She provided inspiration and prophecy, guidance and leadership, wisdom and skill, renewal and restoration. She was a comforter & helper. She empowered the disciples as "the advocate". And she's a gift giver.

And while all of that is great, I suppose the question can be asked what any of that has to do with love. To answer that let's start in the book of proverbs. In proverbs chapter 8 we find what's written as a quotation from wisdom, for which Sophia is Greek, for describing her part in creation. It says, "the Lord created me at the beginning of his work, the first of his acts of long ago. Ages ago I was set up, at the first, before the beginning of the earth," and continuing in verse 30 "then I was beside him like a master worker; and I was daily his delight, rejoicing before him always, rejoicing in his inhabited world and delighting in the human race." Of course, we know that this aligns with Genesis 1 "In the beginning when God created the heavens and the earth, the earth was a formless void and darkness covered the face of the deep, while a wind of God swept over the face of the waters." And so, while God, the creator, looked upon the earth and all that was created and said it was good, Sophia, delighted in the human race.

In continuing to talk about love, and sticking with words attributed to Solomon, we look to the apocryphal book of the wisdom of Solomon to one of my favorite verses. “Therefore, I prayed, and understanding was given to me; I called on God, and the spirit of wisdom came to me. I loved her more than health and beauty, and I chose to have her rather than light, because her radiance never ceases. All good things came to me along with her, and in her hands uncounted wealth.” He continues in describing her, “there is in her a spirit that is intelligent, holy, unique, manifold, subtle, mobile, clear, unpolluted, distinct, invulnerable, loving the good, irresistible, beneficent, humane, steadfast, sure, free from anxiety, all powerful, overseeing all, and penetrating through all spirits that are intelligent pure and altogether subtle….For God loves nothing so much as the person who lives with wisdom. She is more beautiful than the sun and excels every constellation of the stars. Compared with the light she's found to be superior, for it is succeeded by the night, but against wisdom evil does not prevail…” Find yourself a partner who talks about you the way Solomon talks about the Holy Spirit. Am I right?

For God loves nothing so much as the person who lives with wisdom. Who could not love a being with characteristics like that? It's a level of perfection I know I can only dream of. But then, the expectation isn't for me to be perfect like wisdom, it's for me to seek and live with Wisdom. The expectation is to welcome wisdom. And why shouldn't we? Living with wisdom doesn't require a certain level of intelligence. Living with wisdom doesn't require a certain level of education. Living with wisdom only requires that we set our preconceived notions and stable ignorance’s aside and allow wisdom to help us know truth and be changed by it. Honestly, my confidence in my ability to do that hasn’t seemed to increase any time that I have said that line. After all, admitting that you know nothing is incredibly hard when you have been expected to know so much.

The true love of God, regardless of the member of the Godhead we are talking about, is that God doesn't have to wait for my insecurities and insufficiencies to be dealt with to be worthy of love or grace. I don't have to reach perfection first. John Wesley taught about three types of grace…well more like three checkpoints of grace, Prevenient Grace, Justifying Grace, and Sanctifying Grace.

Prevenient Grace is the grace that prepares us to hear the gospel and respond. Justifying Grace is momentary, it carries us from the point of unbelief to belief, and Sanctifying Grace continues to work in us, transforming our lives. And Sophia, the bringer of grace, the wisdom of God, in perhaps the most amazing act of love, accompanies us through all of those points.

Before we believe, before we knew what we didn't belief, she was at work in our hearts. The wisdom that she brings with her leads us to a point of understanding that there is more. She patiently waits for us to be ready to discover God and to build that relationship with them. And then through that point of justification and on to sanctification, her wisdom continues to help us grow. And that is what love is. It's standing by the one you care for, providing inspiration, care, patience, guidance, and wisdom until you are able to reach your own conclusions.

All that the Holy Spirit is, all that she is described as doing, all that she has done shows us God's love. You and I have been accompanied through every moment, first breath to last, by God in the Holy Spirit. The same spirit who breathed life into Adam, and helped conceive Jesus. The same spirit who descended as tongues of fire onto the gathered disciples. History has happened in her breath and decisions made under her wise tutelage. She walks with us and waits for the moment we seek her. Because, if God loves the person who lives with wisdom, then all we've left to do is accept that love that's freely offered especially at Christmas time and realize that whether we look for it or not love is actually all around.

Ordinary Time

Overcoming Tā piǎn and Fighting Off Fear

By: Reverend Caroline Morrison
Reading: Psalm 71:1-4, 9-13, 18-19, 24

Theme: God gives us shelter to rest and empowers us to live fearlessly in the face of our enemies.

Over the course of my life, I have been privileged to travel to 4 of the seven continents. My parents gifted me with a love of learning about other cultures and their history. So, when my father was stationed in Germany we didn't stay on post. We traveled around the country and around Europe visiting Roman ruins, castles, former Nazi bunkers and sights, and Dachau Concentration camp. We shopped the markets, ate food and I picked up some German along the way. Not much mind you, like I told the patient the other day “Ich spreche ein bitchen deutsche”. Which means that I speak a little German. My children will tell you that I will occasionally use phrases like ‘was willst du zu essen?’ which means ‘what do you want to eat?’ and small things I remember.

I tend to pick up different phrases in the different countries that I travel to almost like souvenirs. When I was in Iraq I learned some Arabic. For example, the traditional greeting is “As-salamu alaykum.” And the response is “wa alaykum as-salam”. Which roughly translates to the peace of Allah be with you and also with you. Though I will admit that perhaps my most used Arabic phrase is “inshallah” which we would translate colloquially as ‘if the good Lord's willing and the creeks don't rise.’ If it's God's will that it happens, then it will happen

When I lived in Djibouti, I began to pick up French because it had been a French colony. Mostly hello and goodbye. While preparing for the sermon in which I talked about the movie “The Walk” I learned the French phrase, “Les carottes sont cuites” …or the carrots are cooked. It’s a colloquialism meaning the situation is hopeless. Once the carrots are cooked, there is no uncooking them.

Recently I have been learning French because my son wanted to learn French. I've been using the program Duolingo. I found it interesting that I learned the phrase Je travaille beaucoup, which means I work a lot before I learned the phrase, Je suis la femme d'Jacqueline which means I am Jacqueline's wife. I don't know if it's just an American bias or what, it just seemed a strange learning order.

But, collecting little bits and pieces of languages seems to be something that I just kind of do. And so, like many Americans when TikTok went offline last weekend, I started picking up some Chinese phrases and I would like to teach you a couple today. So, repeat after me, are tong tee pee fa. A rough translation of that phrase is "and the whole body is tired." Les carottes sont cuites are tongtee peefa…the situation is hopeless and the whole body is tired. Ready for the next word I found? "Tā pian" and that has no good English translation. It captures a profound sense of emotional, physical, and mental exhaustion, often tied to relentless pressure or adversity.

When I found that, I was looking for something that could describe what I was experiencing and physical, mental, and emotional exhaustion just didn't seem strong enough. So, tā piǎn.

Friends, did you know it's only been a week since the inauguration? It felt so much longer. It seemed that Monday started an onslaught that just kept coming with something new every day. Every time I turned around there was another attack being lobbed over the walls of the margins focused on someone else. As I sat down to write this, I found out about the memorandum from Secretary of State Marco Rubio stopping the processing of passports for all transgender people. Birthright citizenship, immigration raids, personhood at conception, trans identities erased…by Wednesday…tā piǎn.

I have cried until there were no more tears. I asked why…I sat in shock. I dissociated. And I tried to write a sermon for today.

I read and re-read the reading for this morning, trying to make some connection. Trying to hear the whisper of Sophia giving me words for this, and, they just weren't there.

Tā piăn. The body of every marginalized community, and each marginalized person within them, Tā piăn. I don't know about you, but, frankly, I'm tired of being tired. I'm tired of being scared. I'm tired of this hopeless, helpless dread that trying to creep over me again. I'm exhausted about the prospect of having to fight again for the rights I already had before I can begin to fight for the rights I was fighting to secure. I am tired of us having to fight for the unalienable rights of life, liberty, and the pursuit of happiness of which we were supposedly endowed by our creator. Tā piăn...you're gonna leave here knowing that word if nothing else.

Now in the army when you're confronted with indirect, or direct, fire the first thing you do is seek shelter. The second thing you do is assess the situation. And then you make a plan. And you follow through on that plan. While sometimes that plan is that you attack, more often than not someone is on the radio to higher headquarters requesting help.

And so, I read through the psalm, again. Only this time I saw something different. You see I was coming at this reading having read through various scholarly interpretations. I had read through this coming from various commentaries. And many of the scholars focused on the age of the psalmist. That this was an older David toward the end of his reign calling on his faith, calling on God.

I had a hard time connecting because despite the aches and the creaks and the snaps and crackles and pops of my joints and my bones, I'd like to think that I'm not old yet. Of course, my kids like to helpfully remind me that might not be reality. But then I realized the psalmist wasn't just writing about being attacked in old age. The psalmist was calling on God to help hold off attacks in general.

The psalmist had reached the point of tā piǎn. He knew it was time to call into higher. In you oh Lord I take refuge let me never be put to shame in your righteousness deliver me and rescue me incline your ear to me and save me. Be to me a rock of refuge, a strong fortress, to save me, for you are my rock and my fortress. Rescue me, oh my god, from the hand of the wicked, from the grasp of the unjust and the cruel.

The song, El Shaddai, says age to age you're still the same. How beautiful is it that we can call upon the same God in this time that the psalmist did? How incredible that we can still depend on the support and love of the creator of this reality? Be to me a rock of refuge. Rock of ages, Cleft for me, let me hide myself in thee. This first part isn't about an attack. This first part isn't really about those out to get David. It is a free and open cry to God. A passionate cry to his creator to be his safe space just like just like God always was.

The string that runs throughout this whole reading is faith and hope. A faith born of all of the things God has done, and a hope that God will care for him in the future. Do not cast me off in the time of old age; Do not forsake me when my strength is spent. God do not forsake me, tā piǎn.

In this this central part of the reading he's pleading to God to not just be a source of refuge for him in the attacks in general. He says over and over God you've been with me from my youth, do not forsake me until I proclaim your might to all the generations to come your power and your righteousness, oh God, reach the high heavens. You who have done great things, oh God, who is like you?

As the reading goes on David is no longer seeking refuge. David's cries for retribution seemed to vanish until the very end of the reading. Instead, he just continues to focus on the great things God has done in his life. He focuses on the ways that God has protected him. He focuses on the ways that God has remained faithful time and time again. Even when he wasn't faithful, God was faithful. And when he falls, God will continue to bring him up. Until finally he says all day long my tongue will talk of your righteous help, for those who tried to do me harm have been put to shame, and disgraced. History has its eyes on them…and no one mourns the wicked.

If God is for us who can be against us. If we spend our life looking at the light, then the darkness is not so easily distracting. When tā piǎn, it is very easy to lose hope. And when the whole body is tired, allowing your faith to shake as you're greeted with wave after wave of attacks is the easiest thing to do. Fear is the greatest inhibitor of joy. Fear will shake your faith and rob you of all hope. It was fear that made Peter deny Jesus three times. It was fear that distracted Peter on the water. And it is fear that keeps us cowering undercover rather than remembering to call on higher.

Friends, fear is a vicious master. It only exists to rob you of your power. It exists to keep you exhausted and hopeless, so you have less likelihood to rise up and fight back. But, fear, never stands against the power of our living, loving, God. Fear kept me in my closet. God empowered me to break it apart and use the wood for kindling at the altar of my soul and so help me, fear will not rebuild that which God has torn down.

God empowers each of us to be ourselves and stands with us in our authenticity. While we may hide in our upper rooms, the spirit continues to prepare us and work on us to help us to pour out the doors sharing the gospel that is written on our hearts.

My beloved siblings, I'm not saying that you can't fear. I'm not saying that you can't be afraid of all that is happening around us and too us. Just that we mustn't allow the fear to blind us from the glory of a God working through the hurt and pain. Take this time, seek cover under God from our enemies just as David did. Fortify yourself for the fight ahead. Focus your sight on the beauty that God has brought upon you in your life. The gifts you have received and the love of God that continues to be there for you, and may you also find a restful respite that you might be rejuvenated and ready to fight the fear being laid before us.

The Inverse Property of Social Equity

By: Reverend Caroline Morrison

Reading: Luke 6:17-26 (The Sermon on the Plains)

Theme: Social Prosperity Requires Equity

I have officially reached the point in my youngest son's life where we are at the limits of my mathematical knowledge. I'm no longer looking things up to make sure I'm showing him the same procedures as his teachers are, I now look them up to try to remember how to do them at all. Luckily, Jacqueline knows more about math than I will ever forget, and she tends to be the one helping him, but, those times I have helped I was pleased to realize that even with my limited knowledge, there are some things that I still remember.

At this moment he is doing algebraic equations and solving for the variable. And I know enough to know about the inverse property of mathematics to be intimidating. How many of you remember the inverse property of mathematics? The inverse property of mathematics simply states that when an operation is performed on a number and its inverse, the result is the original number or a neutral element. So, for example, if you have three, and you take away three...you are left with 0 a neutral element. If you are multiplying by three and you divide by three, you are left with 1, and so on...So, with that in mind...Let's talk about Luke's beatitudes.

The reading in Luke today is commonly called the Sermon on the Plains. If it feels familiar, it's because it's the Sermon on the Mount 2.0. This pericope is commonly referred to as the beatitudes, and it's always bothered me for some reason. It just seemed to be doublespeak. Don't misunderstand me, I am one that loves symmetry. And the general symmetry of the Beatitudes is beautiful. Practically fold it in half and you have positives and negatives just right there lined up perfectly.

But there is something that bothers me about some of these. And I was never quite able to put my finger on it. I knew the dichotomy made them something to be studied and they shouldn't be taken at just face value.

Blessed are you who are poor but woe to you who are rich. Blessed are you who are hungry now for you will be filled but woe to you who are filled now for you will be hungry. So, if you're hungry you're going to be filled and then once you're filled, you'll be hungry. It seemed almost like a self-fulfilling prophecy or something. If you're laughing now you will cry, and if you're crying now, you'll laugh. Do you see the cycle? All of them read kind of like that.

And then of course we get to the blessing on the persecuted. This blessing was drilled into me as a Baptist. It was expected that you would annoy people enough as a Christian that they would hate you. The persecution complex within evangelical Christianity is a very real thing. It's why sometimes you'll hear about the persecution of Christians in America when Christianity is the most privileged religion in the world, let alone the country. At the same time, it's a very strange place to be put in when you've been taught to be a people pleaser who is supposed to be persecuted and hated. There's a tumultuous dichotomy that exists in that cultural expectation.

But, that wasn't even it, and then, it hit me. I don't know if it's because of Zaccheaus' math or what, but, the inverse property of mathematics fits here...call it the inverse property of social equity. The reason they bothered me is because the entire reading cancels itself out. It seems like a waste of air because the positive and negative hit each other and result in a neutralizing effect where everyone is the same. There is no rich or poor...just the middle...the satisfied. I mean, can you imagine not really having possessions...no need for greed or hunger...a siblinghood of humanity. Imagine all the people just sharing all the world. I know...John Lennon was amazing right? Who knew he put the beatitudes to song??

The inverse property of social equity has also come to mind thinking of the Apostle Paul and his writing to the Galatians. I've been thinking of them and a world of no labels… "There is no longer Jew or Greek, there is no longer slave or free, there is no longer male and female; for all of you are one in Christ Jesus."

The Beatitudes can largely be boiled down to the same outcome. If you break them down, they leave us with a society where we truly are equal. Not that we aren't diverse…we do still have the image of God within us after all. We are still beautifully different, but, those differences don't make us better or worse than anyone else. It's a divine DEI program of which we are all a product. DEI of course is the latin word Dei meaning, God. All of us are bearers of the imago Dei…the image of God.

Patterns of oppression are gone. Privilege is no longer a thing, because we're all actually equal. Social prosperity requires that equity, and, truly knowing the Kindom of God requires it as well. You see the inverse property of social equity works because no one person is trying to be better than another. No one person is trying to have a leg up on another. Our goal in a society that is governed by the inverse property of social equity is that we work to more fully commune with each other and thereby with God.

Now you might be thinking this sounds an awful lot like socialism. And that's because in many ways it is. Jesus preferred economy is socialist. And even worse his preferred government isn't a constitutional republic…it's a socialist monarchy. As we have talked about before, that has always been the intention of God. Our capitalist ideals in this country, and our supposed belief in democracy, keep us from actually achieving that though. And there are multiple threads that go throughout Scripture; the love of God is one of the threads, another is God as king.

In a modern context we've really lost the idea of what a king truly is. Even going back to the 1700s, the monarchy that we learn about was not an absolute power over the government. Rather, the monarchy in Britain was a unitary parliamentary constitutional monarchy. Meaning power was in a centralized government, executive power is with the parliament elected by the people, and the monarch shares power but is largely a figurehead.

Because that is what our primary context for a monarchy is and that is often what we relegate God to…a figurehead. Jesus is King of Kings and Lord of Lords…and yet, Christians have a bad habit of ignoring the simplest of edicts. Our experience of a king is not the sacred kingship of ancient Egypt or the ancient Israelites, our experience of a monarchy is Great Britain.

And, I have news for you the monarchy of Great Britain is not what the monarchy of God is supposed to be. You see the inverse property of social equity, this idea that all of us can be equal if we care for one another requires the existence of a benevolent king who provides for us just as the ravens and lilies of the field are provided for to the point we don't worry about our needs. To reach the point where the beatitudes actually run their course and social equity is a thing that truly does exist, we have to reach a point where our only want is to use the gifts and talents God has given us to enhance the praise we have, and experience we have for God. To join God in caring for creation and making it more beautiful.

The reality is that such a drastic change is not something that is just going to happen. It is something that takes time and intentional practice. It's a change that needs to be built to. Which is evidenced by the fact that we have been trying to build to it for centuries. In 1789 John Wesley delivered a sermon called the use of money. And in it he first uttered the now famous words "earn all you can, save all you can, and give all you can." He said that if Methodists would give all they can, then all would have enough.

It's a beautiful dream, mind you. But in a society like we have today it's still just that. It is still just a dream. And the crazy thing about this not being able to come fruition so easily is that unlike simply giving everything, John Wesley's plan encourages comfort. If we're comfortable, then we don't want. We are satisfied. And so, earn as much as you can to be comfortable now, save all that you can so that you're comfortable in the future, and give all that you can so that others may be comfortable too. I understand that this isn't a Methodist congregation, but then, John Wesley wasn't a Methodist (they didn't start the denomination until after his death), he was an Anglican priest and is now an Episcopal saint.

But the dream of a beatitude's community, A Kingdom of God on earth, a socialist monarchy where we are all the equal, diverse subjects of our benevolent creator is one that we should still continue to strive for today. And so, my friends, I encourage you as we move toward the Lenten season, to start living into that beatitude's community. Find the equilibrium of a satisfied existence. One where needs are met, wants are fulfilled, and everything left is given to others so that existence may be true for them as well. You may say it's dream, but, I'm not the only one who has had it. And, I hope and pray you will have it as well and the world can live as one beautiful, beatitudes community.

A Love Without End, Amen

By: Reverend Caroline Morrison
Reading: 1 Corinthians 13:1-13

Theme: Love is the not-so-secret ingredient.

On March 2, 2025, the blockbuster musical Wicked will see if it can do what its predecessor was unable to a little more than 20 years prior at the 2004 Tony Awards. Much like 2024 and 2004 seemed dominated by the musical Wicked. It starred Kristen Chenoweth, who had charmed audiences with her performance as Sally in the musical You're a Good Man, Charlie Brown and of course, the wickedly talented, one and only Idina Menzel who originated the role of diva-extraordinaire, Maureen Johnson in the musical Rent. They went into the award season in 2004 with everyone expecting Wicked to walk away with the award for best musical. Instead, the 2004 Tony Award for best new musical went to the musical Avenue Q.

If you've never heard of Avenue Q don't worry, you probably aren't alone. Nowadays, wicked is definitely the bigger of the two musicals. It's had a bit more staying power and that's probably because songs like defying gravity have become part of the zeitgeist and the story of Elphaba is one that so many of us identify with.

Avenue Q was created by a group of former employees at Sesame Street. And Avenue Q was an adult version of Sesame Street. It included real people mixed with puppets and had songs like "purpose" from which I personally draw inspiration fairly regularly. The musical opens with the song "what do you do with a BA in English" as the protagonist is trying to find somewhere to live and realizing that his prospects with a Bachelor of Arts in English seem pretty low. And of course, who could forget the song "Schadenfreude?"

Now, I want to make clear, I never meant to do a sermon series where I teach foreign words and phrases, but, apparently, here we are. So, Schadenfreude is a compound German word comprised of the words Schaden meaning Damage or Harm and Freude meaning Joy. When put together, you get a word for which there is no direct English translation. It roughly translates to happiness at the misfortune of others. Television shows like Wipe-Out and America's Funniest Home Videos capitalize on the existence of Schadenfreude.

It's a key part of who we are as humans. Especially today, Friedrich Nietzsche suggested that the emotional pain people feel about their in groups inferiority results in the pleasure of schadenfreude when its successful outside group fails. Schadenfreude is born out of a sense of envy. And it's the opposite of sympathy. It's thought to be closely linked to what's called the dark triad traits so apparently in psychology there's the dark triad traits and the light triad traits. The dark triad traits are narcissism, Machiavellianism, and psychopathy. The light triad traits are humanism, faith in humanity, and Kantianism which is the ultimate principle of morality.

The truth is schadenfreude is built into the human experience now because we often misunderstand what love truly is. 1 Corinthians 13:4-8 has become so ubiquitous and overused in weddings that much like the vows that are spoken shortly after them, people don't pay much attention to them and what they truly mean. People don't go in depth with them. People definitely don't go in depth with the verses surrounding it.

“If I speak in the tongues of mortals and of angels but don't have love, I am a noisy gong. If I have prophetic powers and understand all mysteries and if I have all faith so let's move mountains but do not have love, I'm nothing. If I give away all my possessions, and I hand over my body so that I may boast but do not have love, I gain nothing.” You can do everything that Jesus says you should but if you don't do it out of love then it doesn't actually mean anything. Love is the ingredient that makes everything worth it. You'll recall that we talked months ago of Jesus saying to love your enemies and pray for those who persecute you. With all of the hurt and harm that we've been feeling as a community recently how often have, we thought to love our enemies even as we fear their actions?

As Jesus hung upon the cross, he prayed according to Luke “…Father, forgive them; for they do not know what they are doing.” That's what love really looks like. The reading today is often painted solely as an example of what love looks like, but Paul is writing this list because that love is missing from the church. They're doing the right things for the wrong reasons. The Christianity isn't working right because they keep forgetting to include love.

Paul is saying everything else comes easy compared to love. Speaking in tongues, moving mountains, giving away everything and handing over your body is simple. But doing it out of love? That's the challenging thing because having selfish ulterior motives is often second nature.

Thanks to Paul, we know what love is. He gives us the now cliched list: “love is patient, kind, neither envious, boastful, arrogant, or rude. It is not insistent on its own way. It's not irritable or resentful. And it does not rejoice in wrongdoing. It bears all things, believes all things, hopes all things, endures all things, and survives beyond all things.” That sounds really familiar, doesn't it?

Paul's lists are amazing after all. See when I read through what love is in the letter to the Corinthians, I'm reminded of the fruits of the spirit we find it in the letter to the Galatians. If you don't remember the fruits of the spirit, they are “love, joy, peace, patience, kindness, goodness, faith, gentleness, and self-control.” He says in that letter “if we live by the spirit, come and let us be guided by the spirit. Let us not become conceited, competing against one another, envying one another.”

Which is easiest do you think? To love, or, to envy? Truthfully, it's easiest to envy. It's easiest to look at another person and imagine that it's so much easier for them and to want to have what they do. There is nothing easy about love. That's why schadenfreude exists, because it's easier to find happiness in the downfall of someone else than it is to find happiness in the struggle to love the person we envy. Love is supposed to be something that we embody. It is supposed to be something that is so powerful, it's second nature to us. But I want to do something. I want you to close your eyes and I'm going to reread verses 4 through 8 from the reading today with one slight change. See if you can pick out the change.

I am patient. I am kind. I am not envious, or boastful, or arrogant, or rude. I do not insist on my own way. I am not irritable or resentful. I do not rejoice in wrongdoing, but, I rejoice in truth. I bear all things. I believe all things. I hope all things. I endure all things. Open your eyes. Love for those that call themselves Christian is a fruit of the Spirit. It is something that is supposed to be so embodied by us that it's second nature. And yet, if you're anything like me then putting myself into the definition of what love is becomes very problematic.

Because, while I may not rejoice in wrongdoing, I do experience schadenfreude. I can be very resentful. And I can be incredibly envious. Galatians does have another list in it and that's the works of the flesh: "fornication, impurity, licentiousness, idolatry, sorcery, and enmities, strife, jealousy, anger, quarrels, dissensions, factions, envy/murder, drunkenness, carousing…etc." It's not an exhaustive list. Some of the works of the flesh definitely appear in my life far more than love.

"When I was a child, I spoke like a child, I thought like a child, I reasoned like a child; When I became an adult I put an end to childish ways. For now, we see in a mirror, dimly, but then we will see face to face. And now faith, hope, and love abide, these three; And the greatest of these is love." There are few things quite as insulting as being called childish. But that's what's happening here. I stopped being a child when I became an adult. I stopped thinking like a child, I stopped reasoning like a child, I stopped speaking like a child, I stopped acting like a child.

To envy, to be impatient, to insist on your own way, those are childish. Those are things we should grow out of as we grow in our relationship with Jesus. Is schadenfreude so enjoyable that we would rather keep that then learn to show love? It does feel a little ironic preaching this to those from communities under attack, but the truth is that the expectation to love is not just an expectation of those with power. It is also from the powerless. Jesus expected the people of Israel to love the Romans just as much as he expected the Romans to love the people of Israel; the marginalized are expected to love those in power just as much as those in power are expected to love the marginalized.

For most of us, the closest we get to love when we look at those we see as adversaries is tolerance. I tolerate people that helped bring about the situation we're in today. I tolerate people who voted a certain way. I tolerate people who advocate for harm towards communities I am surrounded by. But, tolerance is not love. Nowhere in that list from Paul did it say love is tolerant. Tolerance is not one of the fruits of the spirit. Jesus didn't say that we should tolerate our enemies. Tolerance is not Christian. We are called to one thing as followers of Christ and that is love. We are called to the hardest thing possible so let's look at how to get from tolerance to love. There are 5 steps to move from tolerance to love. Not 12, although each one of these five steps has 2 sub steps and so I guess there $A = \pi r^2$ technically 10 steps. You know what? The math doesn't matter, there's a path.

Step one: awareness and acceptance. As with anything, we have to admit that there's a problem. Not only do we have to admit that there is a problem, we have to admit our part in the problem. I think that too often we focus on the reality that there is a problem without the accountability that comes from how we help perpetuate that problem. And so, we have to have times of self-reflection. We have to recognize our own biases and prejudices. As I drive around northeast Kansas, I see political signs and flags all over the place. And I feel inside me anger, and resentment, and judgment. All those are signs that point to love, right? No. Those point to my own biases and prejudices.

And so there must be some self-reflection where I'm able to admit the biases and prejudices I have. You also educate yourself. You learn about diverse cultures and experiences. If you learn about the people that are opposite, you on various issues you start finding out that they're not all evil. There are some people that are evil in their intentions and actions, but the vast majority aren't.

It's estimated that as many as 50% of troops did not fire their weapons in the early years of World War 2 because they still saw their enemy as human. And so, there was a major propaganda push to dehumanize the enemy. That happens in modern politics as well. Nearly every person in this room has been dehumanized and has been painted with a broad brush as some type of enemy at some point in history, if it's not happening right now. And if we look at the other side, we often paint them with the same broad strokes. They are ignorant, hateful bigots. And yet, when you chip away the paint from the brush stroke, you start realizing that that's not actually the case. They are just as monolithic as you are.

Step 2 is tolerance. Because you can't even start with tolerance when you're moving away from tolerance. And so, Step 2 is the beginning of that movement. The two sub steps are respect differences and have positive interactions. We've got to start practicing accepting and respecting differences of other people even if we don't understand them. We expect people to respect our differences. Tolerating is respecting their differences and their right to have differing opinions and differing ideas. Even if they aren't based in science. Even if they aren't factual. That person that believes that we did not go to the moon and that the earth is flat has a right to believe that. The person that believes trans people don't exist has a right to believe that. And we can respect that right, while disagreeing with their stance. We also need to not only engage in adversarial interactions. Those are the easy ones to have. The debates with the haters and people that are against our existence, those are easy to find. But positive interactions require intentionality. Having interactions that don't just divide us but instead bring us together, requires us to be intentional that we're going to have those interactions. It requires us to accentuate the positive rather than allowing us to always be consumed by the negative.

Step 3 is empathy. We have to listen to others with an open heart and mind and imagine what it would be like to be in someone else's situation. I said months ago that on both sides of the last election there was fear. It was the common denominator in why people voted both ways. The average person voted that way because they were afraid something would get worse, and they wanted things to be better. Being able to acknowledge that commonality is important. When we find reasons for us to be with each other it's harder for those in power to divide us.

Step 4 is connection and compassion. Form genuine connections with other people and act with kindness and compassion. Forming genuine connections with others requires that we see people as individuals. Genuine connections means that I can see God in you. Forming genuine connections with other people means that they become other people. It means that I'm not othering them even if they are othering me. Because we're supposed to do unto others as we would have them do unto us. If I am othering them that I am not treating them the way I want to be treated. If I am not showing them kindness and compassion regardless of how they're acting towards me, then I am not reflecting God.

Once you've gone through awareness and acceptance, tolerance, empathy, and connection and compassion, the last step is love. Practice unconditional love by loving others for who they are without judgment or conditions. Spread positivity by sharing love and positivity with others. That unconditional love is what tends to get us. It's a lot easier to love someone if they love us back. It's a lot easier to love someone if they didn't show hate to you first. But unconditional love is exactly that. Unconditional love doesn't require you to love me. According to Andrew Lloyd Webber, you must love Eva Peron; but, you don't have to love me.

That's it. Moving from tolerating someone to loving them is really simple, isn't it? No. It's not. No one said it would be. There's nothing about that list of what love is that is easy for any one of us to do. But the struggle to love, to learn to love unconditionally, is the struggle to shake free of our human failings in favor of our divine birthright. You and I are holders of the image of God, we are children of God. From our very creation we are loved, and we are called by God to love others. The world teaches us about the satisfaction of schadenfreude, but God teaches us that the true secret ingredient to happiness and joy and peace and satisfaction in this life is love.

Head, Shoulders, Knees & Toes

By: Reverend Caroline Morrison
Reading: 1 Corinthians 12:12-27

Theme: Equality in Diversity

I used to have a pretty big issue with Paul's use of the human body as an illustration and that's partly due to the fact that I have a love/hate relationship with Paul. As I have studied, however, I've come to understand that it's less an issue with Paul, as it is an issue with the gross misuse and misinterpretation of Paul's writing. I still believe that one of the worst things they did when creating the cannon was including the Epistles. There's no need for them to be in Scripture. But then, that's really my issue.

When it came to the body, I wasn't convinced that the best way to talk about the church was in relation to the Human body. I mean the human body is amazing, don't get me wrong. For example, did you know the human brain can hold five times as much information as any encyclopedia on the earth? Scientists estimate that the human brain can probably store around 1000 terabytes of data, though I'm not sure that mine can. Or how about that the acid in your stomach is strong enough to dissolve razor blades. The strongest muscle in the body isn't the heart of the lungs, it's the tongue. And the final fun fact about the body that I have for you today is that on average, our bodies give off enough heat in 30 minutes to bring half a gallon of water to boil though, that doesn't quite explain why I'm always dying of heat while my wife has curled up under a blanket.

But despite all of those incredible facts and all of the others that exist, the truth is the body is limiting. The human body breaks down really easily sometimes for reasons that aren't understood. There is sickness, and cancer. There are so many little things I could think of and yet the more I thought, the more I started to realize just how perfect an analogy the human body really might be.

One thing you can count on when it comes to Paul is a repetition of ideas. The idea of the body of Christ Is one that we find repeated in the letter to the church in emphasis and, the letter to the Romans. Now of course none of them are identical. That would just be way too easy. But while the Specific words and even focus might be a little bit different the overarching message remains the same and it can be summed up using the initialism DEI.

Interestingly enough it comes fairly close to meaning exactly what you think it does. In a modern sense DEI is diversity, equity, and inclusion. When discussing Paul's body theology, however, its diversified unity, equality, and Interdependence. So, let's look at the first one, diversified unity.

In all three of the letters Paul makes it very clear that because of Christ we are one. The differences that are ascribed to us by society cease to exist. The privileged disparity and power differentials ceased to exist. Specifically, in the reading today, He says we were all baptized into one body, Jews or Greeks, slaves or free.

Next, we have equality and care. Paul made it very clear all members should have equal concern for each other. If one part of the body of Christ suffers every part suffers with it, if one is honored every part rejoices. The body is a system. If one part of the system isn't working it messes up other parts. At the same time, if a part of the body isn't working properly, other parts work to compensate. We've all heard that if we lose our eyesight that our other senses kick in to compensate for that loss. It works the same for most injuries. The body parts are symbiotic. They're connected and they live in a delicate balance. Something as simple as potassium being off can make everything out of whack.

Finally, we have interdependence which is the idea that each member of the church relies on the others. The well-being of one affects the well-being of the whole. Regardless of the location of the church, the governing of the church, according to Paul is designed to be socialist monarchy which is in keeping with the teachings of Jesus as we discussed before. Jesus was very clear that you give unto Caesar what is Caesar's, and you give unto God that which is God's. Meaning that there should be separation a recognition of the earthly government and a serving of the divine monarchy in the church. That Socialist monarchy should see us caring for one another and relying on one another for everything from inspiration to emotional support.

The church, much like the human body, benefits from the diversity of its systems and design, but, there are certain needs that are often neglected in its care. The human body has need for recreation and so does the church. Too often our churches fall into the trap of treating the mission of the church as a divine responsibility devoid of celebration. We focus so much on justice and the work, that we forget to take the time to enjoy this life. Even moments of enjoyment are often treated as part of the mission. We plan community cookouts but that's never just about fellowship with our neighbors there's a motive to bring them inside the walls. Even Jesus took time for recreation and fun. His first miracle was at a wedding after all.

The human body has a need for self-care and so does the church. Jesus demonstrated it for us. We've talked about the importance of self-care before reaching burnout. We've talked about the importance of taking space to breathe. The same exists for the body of the church. It cannot truly take care of the world unless we're taking care of it also. We have to make sure that our church body is kept just as healthy, or healthier, as our human body. And sometimes that does mean closing the doors for a minute and letting the members breathe and meditate.

The human body has a need to dream and to hope and so does the church. Sometimes, we get so focused on the here and now that we forget to dream about what we hope is to come. If we have faith that God will take care of us, and hope for a brighter future then we can find joy today.

But just like with our body, the very things that keep us going are often the things we neglect to do. Who has time for recreation when there is so much fight that needs to happen? Who has time for the self-care of the church when there are communities that are quite literally under attack? What body has time to rest when there's so much that needs to be done? The church has the same problem that the humans in charge of it often do. In our case it's a lack of work life balance and in so many ways it's killing the church of today.

In verse 26, Paul says, "if one member suffers, all suffer together with it; if one member is honored, all rejoice together with it." God bless the dichotomies. The body of Christ needs to rest sometimes. When all you do is spend your time fighting the adversity in front of you and you spend no time in Fellowship with your fellow body parts and with the creator of that body, there can be no refreshment. We go into the fight at a disadvantage because we haven't allowed ourselves to take care of ourselves.

So, at this time, We're going to have some fun. We are going to take a second and recall the joy we felt when we were kids in children's church. I want you to stand as your able and we are going to take a couple of minutes to care for ourselves.

Sing: He's Got the Whole World In His Hands & Head, Shoulders, Knees, and Toes…followed by a minute of silent breathing.

The other thing we really need to focus on is that in the body of Christ, in the group or collection that is the church, Dei. The diversity, equality, and interdependence. God has given each one of us gifts and talents for ministry. That diversity is not just social status or race or gender or sexuality.

That diversity lay in the collection of gifts and talents that we have. As Paul says shortly after this reading, God has appointed in the church, first apostles, second prophets, third teachers; then deeds of power, gifts of healing, forms of assistance, forms of leadership, various kinds of tongues. He says not everyone is meant to do everything. Just like an eye can't be swapped for a kidney, a person with a gift for preaching may not have a gift for administration. A person with a gift for teaching youth may not have a gift for teaching children.

I remember when I was going through the RCIA process to become Catholic we used to joke that one of the requirements to become a priest was that you couldn't carry a tune. It seemed like every priest that got up during a mass just tried really hard but that simply wasn't where their gift lay. So, knowing your gift is extremely important.

How many churches have we seen where the same people have been doing the same job for years and years because they have a gift? At one point, I was the lay ministry coordinator for First Lutheran Church here in Topeka and finding volunteers to take part of new things was next to impossible. And so, it always seemed to fall on the exact same people every time until they were burned out.

Just like our bodies can learn to not rely on muscle memory and be able to do anything sometimes that means allowing ourselves to better refine our secondary gifts. For the longest time, the primary gift I used in church was music. I sang in the choir, I sang special music, I sang for different events at the church. When Jacqueline and I met, I was getting paid to sing in the church choir First United Methodist Church in El Dorado.

Preaching wasn't necessarily a gift I knew I had until the first time I did it. When I lost my church and we came back to Topeka, I returned to music. And I thank God every time I have an opportunity to use the gift of preaching that I've been given. Learning to recognize the diversity in our own gifts, as well as in the gifts of the people in the church, is the only way to avoid burnout in both places.

To best accomplish our mission, we have remembered we are equal to one another. I have seen the trappings of social status be brought into the hierarchy of the church too often. Footloose, the story of the pastor who terrorized the youth of a small midwestern town by imposing his bible-backed will before being beaten by dance, was based on a true story after all. And, let's be honest Rome is beautiful. The Vatican, I've heard, is breathtaking. However, I can imagine that Jesus, the socialist monarchist, would not appreciate the opulence of Rome any more now than he did when he was walking around the Earth.

I can imagine that Jesus also wouldn't take kindly to dogmatic divisions among denominations either. Some denominations are so focused on telling people they're wrong, that they forget to tell people they're loved. And some denominations are so focused on loving themselves that they forget they're supposed to love outside the walls too.

In an equal body, we realize we are all drawn together for a reason. Verse 18 says, "but as it is, God arranged the members in the body, each one of them, as he chose. If all were a single member, where would the body be? As it is, there are many members, yet one body."

There is no one church that is the body of Christ. Rather all of us are. Prevenient Grace is brought to each human on this planet. The body of Christ, the Corpus Christi, is all of us. We should be humble enough to depend on one another, and, confident enough to work on each other's behalf. It's important to remember that not only are we all siblings in Christ, and children of God, it's important to remember that we are all members of the same body. All of us here in the sanctuary, everyone joining at home, and everyone around the world. Even those denominations that we don't agree with, they are still partners in this system of ministry.

Sometimes the gifts we need aren't gifts we find in our congregation. Sometimes we experience arguments that split our Congregation. There are two churches in town that exist because one church was built by civil war veterans and wanted to have the flag in the sanctuary and the other didn't. Even the writer of today's reading was part of a major rift. Paul and Peter did not agree on what it took to be Christian in the practicing, practical sense. Did we have to become Jews first or could Gentiles simply be Christian? It quite literally took divine intervention through a dream to finally bring an end to that disagreement.

Just like with the human body, sometimes the parts don't get along. Sometimes white blood cells attack good tissue. Sometimes a nerve gets pinched and causes damage down a leg. Sometimes we have to amputate in order for the rest of the body to be able to function. But with all of that come up it's still the same body. With all of the disagreements that we have, with all of the hate and everything that is to come, It's important to remember that beyond all of our human issues, we are still the body of Christ. And even if parts happen damaged, We can still do our part to ensure that the mission of showing the love of God unto the world is fulfilled and that our little piece of the body of Christ remains active, healthy and engaged.

Holy, Authentic Fire

By: Reverend Caroline Morrison
Reading: 2 Corinthians 3:12-4:2

Theme: We are Controlled Infernos

Pop Quiz time! Who remembers any of the foreign words from the last few sermons? Schadenfreude, "tāpiàn" (踏遍), les carrots sont queet…you didn't think they would come back up did you? Well apparently it's become a theme that I teach a foreign word on the Sundays leading up to lent because I accidentally started doing it. Today's word: bivouac. Bivouac has French roots and while it used to mean night guard, it has since come to mean a temporary campsite used by soldiers and mountaineers. So, there you go, your word for today is bivouac.

When I was in the military, every month or so we would find ourselves in the field, setting up a bivouac site. There was nothing overly fancy about it. There was usually one big tent for command and meetings and then all of us would have our little tents set up around it.

We, of course, had rules for when we were in the field, and I was surprised the day I discovered that some of them are found in scripture. For example, if you have to use the bathroom and you're camped against the enemy you're to go on the outskirts of the camp and dig a hole and then fill the hole in after you've used it because the Lord moves among you in the camp and doesn't want to step in your poop. That's obviously very paraphrased. You're not going to find that in the NRSV or the King James. But it's still very useful. One of the more modern rules is that if you are moving a vehicle in the bivouac site, you needed a ground guide, someone to walk in front of the vehicle, to ensure you didn't accidentally drive over someone. Another is about noise and light discipline.

Now light discipline has always been incredibly important because if you run around with a white light at night, it messes with everyone's night vision. If you do have to use a light, you want it to be a red light. That's the reason why I have my phone set up so if you click the power button three times the screen turns red. If I get up in the middle of the night to do something I want to still maintain some night vision.

But, with the advent of night vision goggles, there arose another, more pressing reason for light discipline. When you are in the field the smallest spark can be picked up by night vision. If you are a smoker you had to be really careful because that little end of the cigarette would be picked up from far away. When I was in Iraq, we would sometimes watch Big Marfu and Little Marfu, two tiny towns that weren't far from us, launch small missiles at each other at night through the night vision goggles. You couldn't see it without them but with them you could watch as they went back and forth across the sky.

But, because of the need for safety you became really adept at hiding light so that you didn't become a target. If you must use light, you ducked into a tent or under some type of cover. You covered your watch if the hands glowed. You did everything you could to make sure as little light shone as possible.

With all of the legislation that is being introduced and passing through state legislatures and federal legislatures and being signed with the squiggle in the oval office, the practice of employing light discipline in your daily life, and hiding the light within you, can seem extremely tempting. And I'm not here to tell you that you can't give in to that temptation. Sometimes the need to feel safe can be overwhelming and hiding that light can give us at least the illusion that we are safe for the moment.

I'm reminded of the stories in Genesis of the travels of Abram and Sarai and later Abraham and Sarah. There are a couple of times when, for safety, Abram tells his wife, 'Hey you are absolutely gorgeous, and they will kill me to take you so just tell them you're my sister.' They do this twice and it does not work either time. In both instances she says I'm his sister and the king or the Pharaoh takes her into his house, and it takes God coming to them in their dreams and telling them that it's not okay because she's actually married, in order to ensure nothing happens to Abraham and Sarah.

Even with the power of God on our side, the temptation to hide ourselves, to dim our light, to capitulate to those who would like nothing more than to see us disappear is incredibly strong. The saying is when existence is resistance then I will resist with every breath of my being, but there is an underlying understanding to that, which is when existence is resistance then existence cannot be safe. The fact is that things are not safe for those in marginalized communities. Regardless of which community you are part of, be you queer, immigrant, disabled, poor, a person of color, a woman, or some mixture of them, or something that lay outside of them…Safety is simply hard to find at this point regardless of how much you try to hide your light.

Today is Transfiguration Sunday in the liturgical calendar. It's the day that the Gospel reading in the lectionary is Jesus' meeting on the hilltop with Elijah and Moses. It's the story of the disciples viewing Jesus going from Jesus the grey to Jesus the white, clothed in garments that are so white that they can barely stand to look at him. He glows. He is a light on that mountain top.

Considering that so much of Jesus time on earth is spent telling people not to tell people who he is when they figure it out, the description of this event had to be absolutely mesmerizing to the disciples who were there. But though we celebrate the event…we live in a post transfiguration world. The last time I saw something so extremely white it glowed I was outside in a bathing suit.

And so, the message from Paul today I think fits those that are living in that post transfiguration, even a Post-Pentecost World. I know, the celebration of Pentecost is still a way off on the liturgical calendar, but the event itself is thousands of years in the past. And yet today, you and I are being pressured to hide the light emanating from within us, to snuff out the tongues of flame upon our very heads.

Paul starts out the reading talking about Moses putting a veil over his face to keep the people of Israel from focusing on him; from gazing at him instead of what God has done and said. He says the only way to really see scripture clearly is with that veil removed. I don't know if you've ever tried to do anything with a veil over your eyes, it distorts your vision. It doesn't matter how thin it is, nothing looks quite the same with a veil as it does without one. And how can you expect to see God clearly if you are always looking for God from behind a veil?

He says starting in verse 17, "Now the Lord is the spirit and where the spirit of the Lord is there is freedom. Therefore, since it is by God's mercy that we are engaged in this ministry, we do not lose heart. We have renounced the shameful things that one hides; we refused to practice cunning or to falsify God's word; but by the open statement of truth, we commend ourselves to the conscience of everyone in the sight of God." He goes on in chapter four, verse six to say, "...for it is the God who said let light shine out of darkness who has shown in our hearts to give the light of the knowledge of the glory of God in the face of Jesus Christ."

My beloved siblings, this is one of those times when Paul's words do apply to today. We have renounced the shameful things that one hides; we refused to practice cunning or to falsify God's word. I don't know about you, but at one time I viewed myself as the shameful thing that one hides because I was taught that who I am is something that should be hidden...that it would be more desirable to God to answer my call part-way. That my joy should be in answering my call the way the church and society told me was acceptable.

But my joy is not in who the government allows me to be, and who the church tells me I should be, and who society says I should be, it's found in who God made me to be. The moment we begin to understand that we are not a shameful thing to hide, the closet we are being kept in becomes a chrysalis. And when we emerge, we grow beyond the space in which our souls were bound, and we fly. When we embrace who we are, when we embrace who we were made to be, and not who society has told us we should be, then we are empowered and tasked by our creator to bring that liberation of divine authenticity to everyone who is still locked within their chrysalis. We are empowered to stand firmly in the face of those who would persecute us and blind them with the love shining from within us.

Paul makes it incredibly clear that we're not to hide ourselves. "Let light shine out of darkness." The first command given in creation is "let there be light." And you, and I, and every Christian who has experienced the liberation that comes in knowing our risen Christ, should not be afraid.

Paul says, "we are afflicted in every way, but not crushed; perplexed, but not driven to despair; persecuted, but not forsaken; struck down, but not destroyed." The breaking of our chains caused a spark, which lit a flame, that no law, no man, no government can make us extinguish or dim. For the God that broke our chains and liberated us, is bigger than any institution created by the hands of humanity. The love of God is bigger than the hate of our neighbors.

The Spirit of God has filled each one of us and we are bearers of the image of a genderful, loving, resilient God. In times when depression is found so easily. When feelings of "tāpiàn" (踏遍), the mental, physical, and emotional exhaustion brought about by constant adversity, seem to be insurmountable, when feelings of schadenfreude are easier to come by than feelings of empathy, when les carrots sont queet and it feels like there is no means of peace and joy in this world, remember that you are not in this alone. You have community, we have a space to recharge, a family of siblings in Christ. Close your eyes…take a breath…feel that Spirit move and bind us together.

It is important, as sharers in this divine authenticity, that we don't allow the darkness of this world to push us back into closets we are too big for. Let me hear you declare I am a child of God. Don't just declare it, believe it, proclaim it! Let it rumble forth from the depths of your soul so loud it shakes the foundations of this building and those who would love to silence you. Say it again! We are Children of God and God loves us! "By this open statement of truth, we commend ourselves to the conscience of everyone in the sight of God!"

We're getting ready to sing one of the most beautiful Christian protest anthems ever put to paper. It doesn't get it's due, Because for some reason we have relegated it to a children's song and given it hand motions. We made it cute, as though that makes it any less powerful.

But as we get ready to sing this, I want you to think about what you're singing. This little light of mine, I'm gonna let it shine. Hide it under a bushel? No! I'm gonna let it shine. Won't let anyone blow it out, I'm going to let it shine. Everywhere we go, we're going to let it shine.

My friends, this is a song of resistance. It is a song of resilience. It's a song where we stand up and we loudly and proudly declare that we will not be silenced, we will not be hidden, and we will not be erased. We are children of God, the creator of this reality, liberated by Jesus, the son of God, and the inferno within our souls has been lit by the Holy Spirit herself, and nothing on this Earth can put it out. So, everyone please stand.

Sing This little light of mine.

Friends, you have such an amazing light in you. Stand…Stand firm and resist and know you are empowered in your resistance. Be as annoying at those birthday candles that won't go out. You are loved and may you never forget you're loved.

Lent

Breaking Our Chains (March 9, 2025)
Oh, My God (March 16, 2025)
We Are One in the Spirit (March 23, 2025)
The Rocks and Stones Will Sing (March 30, 2025)
Off on a Hero's Journey (March 6, 2025)

Breaking Our Chains

By: Reverend Caroline Morrison
Reading: Mark 1:12-13

Theme: Fast from those things that hinder.

One of my favorite things about preparing sermons is the process of research and study that goes into it. I often pick up new and useless trivia during this time. For example, the human body can survive months without food, so long as there is a means of hydration. Without that, the life expectancy drops to days. I also learned that my AI is concerned about the number of times I asked it how long a human body could survive without food and water. I believe it ended our last conversation by asking if there was anything else I needed to talk about, and it said it could give me a list of names if so.

I also learned that the other similar expanse of fasting for 40 days and nights with Moses on Mt. Sinai is understood to be a different type of fasting. Moses is meant to be understood as miraculous. And part of the miracle of Moses 40 days and 40 nights on Mount Sinai is that his form of fasting was no food or water. So, the fact that he even lived the whole 40 days and 40 nights was a miracle. Jesus 40 days and nights weren't meant to be miraculous. It was a spiritual practice that could be practiced by all people and so it is believed that while he abstained from food, he still took in water.

And, even with passages that I have heard my entire life, It always amazes me the different themes and ideas I'm able to pick out. When re-reading them, sometimes there are things that I already knew, but I really didn't realize the significance. And sometimes, it's a reframing. When I was preparing for this Lenten series, I started to notice that there is a set of themes and characteristics that seem to appear through all of the readings over the next 5 weeks in some form or another. They aren't all present in every single one mind you, but at least one or two of them is present in each of the Sunday readings.

Would you like to know what they are? Allow me to present to you the five R's of Lent. The five R's are repent rejuvenate, remember, restore, and reckon. And I had to dig deep to find reckon, because, I quite honestly did not want to have a 5 W's and How or a reading writing and arithmetic situation on my hands.

To repent is to feel deep regrets and make a conscious decision to turn away from an action or choice that you've made. To rejuvenate, in this case, is to renew yourself. To remember is to remember that you are imperfect, you are mortal, and you are loved. To restore is reestablishing your relationship with God and with each other. And to reckon would be to confront the things that hinder you. So again, repent, rejuvenate, remember, restore, and reckon…the five R's of Lent.

Now today's gospel reading doesn't begin to touch on much of anything. The events that are talked about in these two verses are events that take place in 3 of the 4 gospels. And unlike so many things, they actually fall in the same order of events in all three gospels. Jesus is baptized, Jesus goes off into the wilderness for 40 days, and then Jesus begins his ministry. And you may not know this about me given the verses I often choose for readings, and the amount I tend to talk, but, I do enjoy brevity. In this case, however, I think Mark, well, missed the mark. Those three events, the baptism, temptation, and beginning of ministry, they are incredible events, and that order is important because it's not one that we often follow as a people very often?

How many of you remember your baptism? Or if you were Methodist, Catholic, or Episcopalian, or one of the other denominations that baptizes as an infant and then confirms later, how many remember your confirmation? Shortly after those outward signs of inward grace, to borrow from the Methodist Church, a person tends to be on fire. They are floating and ready to change the world. To just get out there.

But, they are often like tinder. They light quickly, they burn brightly, and they burn out just as fast if you don't build a fire around them. And for Jesus, his time in the desert is the time that he's stacking the wood around the burning tinder to make sure the fire keeps going.

In the verses right before today's reading Jesus receives affirmation, acknowledgement, and a claim of parentage from God. "You are my son, the beloved; with you I am well pleased." And right after this amazing experience at his baptism he goes off by himself into the desert. But for a bit more context let's move to one of the other gospels where there's a bit more information about what takes place during the trials of Jesus, because the trials and temptations speak a lot about what we should be doing during Lent.

Now, there are some interesting variations between the tellings in Matthew and Luke. In the book of Matthew, for example, it appears that Jesus fasted 40 days and 40 nights and after those 40 days and 40 nights he was famished and that's when the devil came to tempt him. And so, he was actually in the desert longer. In the book of Luke however the author says that Jesus was tempted for 40 days and when the 40 days was over, he was famished and that's where we get the Reckoning scene between Jesus and the devil.

Now, I always enjoy the little idiosyncrasies between the gospel writers. The small differences in focus and timing of events are what helps us in our belief that they are the accounts of different people with different perspectives and different backgrounds. What should matter more for you, and I today is why those particular things were chosen to tempt Jesus with.

So, what are the three temptations of Jesus? Command the stone to become a loaf of bread, Throw yourself down and the angels will come and bear you up, and I will give you all the glory and authority if you just worship me. Regardless of whether you read Luke's telling or Matthew's telling, they may not agree on the order they took place, but, they agree those are the three.

Both readings have been titled by translators as the temptation of Jesus however in keeping with the 5 R's theme, I look at this as the reckoning of Jesus. It's the confrontation between Jesus and the devil. But of everything the devil could have offered, why those three things?

Because the devil focused on the things that kept Jesus' mind bound to this world. Jesus' spirit was soaring from his baptism, but his body was bound to his fears and uncertainties and needs on this planet. After 40 days and 40 nights of fasting and likely living off of whatever water he was able to find, the Gospels say he was famished. He was famished from a lack of food, a lack of social interactions…a lack of everything.

Thinking of other things was likely a chore for him at that point. And so, the Devil says just make this stone into a loaf of bread. Feed yourself! It's in your power you can end your hunger right now and go back to focusing on everything else.

His physical hunger was becoming more and more of a focus for him and keeping him from focus on his spiritual practice. And he tells the devil, "It's written one does not live by bread alone…" Then comes the next temptation in the reckoning. "If you are the son of God throw yourself down from the pinnacle of the temple, Because it's written that God will command as Angels to protect you, they'll bear you up and you won't dash your foot against a stone."

Now at this point Jesus knows what's to come at the end of his ministry. He knows that he is to be raised again from the dead, but, at first he has to die, and we know from his prayer in the Garden of Gethsemane that the pain involved in that task is something he did not want. He begged God to do anything else if it was possible but if it wasn't then he would fulfill God's will. And so, the devil tests Jesus at this moment to see if when faced with the possibility of great pain Jesus would opt to test God's commitment to him.

And then finally, the Devil shows him all the kingdoms of the world and guarantees him that the kingdoms of the world will give him their glory and he would have authority over all of it he just has to worship the devil. Take a knee. In this moment Jesus is offered a way out of the cross. All the kingdoms of the world would be his. They would glorify him. And he could avoid the pain that comes with death. He could avoid having to die and still have everyone glorify him and still have everyone listen to him and have all of that power. But, it wasn't just about having the power. The resurrection had to happen for victory over death.

Jesus knew that his death was a set point. There was no getting around it. And so as much as he wanted to avoid having to die, he told the devil to go away. And he recovers and heads off to begin his ministry.

The fears and uncertainties of life that Jesus dealt with in the desert are part of what it means to be human. It's a huge part of life that that it's something Jesus reckoned with. Our fears and uncertainties are what keep us bound to this world. Our fears and uncertainties keep us from fully living into the prophetic life that we are called to. They keep us safe. They keep us warm and cozy. Our fears and uncertainties hinder us from the relationship with God that God wants us to have.

And so, Lent should be a time of reckoning. It should be a time where we look at our lives and we confront the things that are getting in the way of us living the life God has called us to. We confront our fears and our uncertainties.

For me, I am working to confront the fear that I'm not good enough. I don't remember the last time that I had a job where impostor syndrome didn't play a role. Even when I'm doing the things I'm called to, things I have been praised for, there's still this nagging voice in the back of my head telling me that I'm not good enough. This feeling makes me believe that someday people are going to realize I don't know what the heck I'm doing. Someday people will figure out that I don't belong where I'm at even though none of that's true. I'm reckoning with the face that I can't focus as well on today as I want because I am so worried about the future. I know that worrying about the future is driving Jacqueline crazy. Worrying about the future has taken up a lot of my time.

The fear and uncertainty of belonging and of the future, and of the things I don't have much control over keep me from really living into what I'm doing. And so, for Lent I am giving up my chains. For length this year I am giving up the chains of fear and uncertainty that I have lived with for so long. The fear and uncertainty that allows me to speak boldly behind a pulpit, but, be a mouse in other areas where my voice could do good.

I invite you to do the same. Jesus came to liberate us. Jesus came to set the captives free. Jesus came to free us from the weights and chains society has put upon us. But accepting that freedom requires us to recognize and release the chains. It requires us to recognize the things that hinder us and reckon with those things.

That is the purpose of these next 40 days. These are your days of reckoning. These are your days to throw aside the chains that Jesus has already freed us from. As we sing this next song may it be with open hearts and open eyes. May we proclaim with all of the truth afforded to us that our chains are gone, and we have been set free. And if something is keeping us holding on to those chains, may we spend this time dealing with those so we can experience the freedom and love that our creator has for us.

Oh, My God!

By: Reverend Caroline Morrison
Theme: Talk Honestly With God

Reading: Mark 14:32-36

The scene in the Garden of Gethsemane is one of my favorite scenes in scripture. I have seen it played out in movies Such as the passion of the Christ where the representation of the devil kind of hauntingly stalks Jesus as he prays. It almost insinuates that Jesus doubt and fear is influenced by the devil. I have seen it portrayed in musicals such as Jesus Christ Superstar. To date, the representation in that musical is probably my favorite telling of this scene. It deeply encapsulates Jesus' devotion to the will of God, as well as his fear and frustration of what's to come. But I did find it interesting while preparing for today that I had never noticed the short line that describes Jesus as becoming distressed and agitated when he talked to Peter, James, and John. Anyone that has talked theology with me, for even a short time, has probably figured out that I love the study of the humanity of Jesus, and this description of him...it was beautiful to me.

But what I absolutely love about this short reading today is the simplicity of Jesus' prayer. When looking through prayers in the Old Testament they often seem to encompass entire chapters of books. They would be grand statements of faith or thankfulness, or judgment or lament. The language would be beautiful and poetic. But, using those as a basis for prayer makes prayer seem daunting.

And so, we attempt to simplify prayer by repeating what Jesus taught us. I would imagine that most of us don't truly think about what we say when we pray the Lord's prayer, other than to try to remember the next word what the next word is so that our neighbor doesn't realize that we completely forgot the Lord's prayer. I mean, do we really want God to forgive us the way we forgive others? I would sincerely hope God would have a lot more grace than I sometimes do.

And while many of us might remember that the Bible says, "...whenever you pray, do not be like the hypocrites; for they love to stand and pray in the synagogues and at the street corners, so they may be seen by others... But whenever you pray, go into your room and shut the door and pray to your father who is in secret; and your father who is in secret will reward you." I would venture to guess that we don't pay as much attention to the next thing Jesus said, "When you are praying, do not heap up empty phrases as the Gentiles do; for they think that they will be heard because of their many words."

When you look at the way that so many people pray, when they do pray, it can be awkward and often embarrassing. Even pastors aren't immune from that feeling. I've always laughed a little bit to myself at the memory of everyone in the room at the district meetings trying to avoid eye contact because no one wanted to be called on to say the prayer to bless the meal or open and close the meeting. Praying in public scares the daylights out of me. If you add in that we often try to put a formality or reverence in our prayers, it's no wonder that we often look to prayer as a last-minute option. We tend to do everything we can before we consciously talk to our creator.

That word conscious is important because you and I subconsciously pray all the time. I bet you have a more active prayer life than you realize. In fact, prayer is built into common reactions and conversations that we have every day. We just often aren't taught to recognize the daily prayerlets and so we don't usually count them as prayers.

If you remember back to last week, I told you that some of the topics over the next 5 weeks would encompass one of the five R's Of Lent, and some would encompass more. Can anyone list what the five R's are from last week? Repent, rejuvenate, remember, restore, and reckon. Would you be surprised to find that prayer is one of those areas that encompasses the majority of the Rs? As a matter of fact, the prayerlets that we subconsciously use in our lives often cover most of the Rs.

God, I really screwed that up. *That is a prayer of repentance.*

Oh my God, I am so tired. *That's a prayer for rejuvenation.*

Jesus, I wish I could just get out of my own way. *That's a prayer of reckoning*

Jesus, take the wheel. *That's a prayer releasing control and restoring your relationship with God.*

In fact, the simpler prayers seem to show-up an awful lot in pop culture and the music that surrounds us. The song *Jesus Take the Wheel*, by Carrie Underwood, was inescapable when it first came out. It was her first country hit and started her country career. We know who she is today largely because of that song. The concept was simple, and relatable. It's the story of turning to prayer at a point where you could no longer do it on your own. Prayer as a last resort. Break glass in case you need God. It's a point in life that I think each of us has been to, when we finally decide that if we can't handle it, we need to just let God do it.

And it takes forever to get to that point because even though we're introduced to the idea of praying as children with 'Now I lay me down to sleep' and 'Bless us O Lord and these thy gifts which we are about to receive from thy bounty through Christ our lord, Amen,' by the time we become older believers we seem to have acquired this idea that prayer needs to look like John 17, grandiose and huge…and we need to all sound like theologians in order for our prayers to be worthy of being heard by God. If you don't at least have $100,000 in student loans for seminary, you don't need to be praying out loud.

But then, if we don't have to sound like we graduated from seminary, then what are the requirements for prayer? According to the parallel reading to the introduction of the Lord's prayer in Matthew, we look to Luke 11. His disciples asked him, "Lord, teach us to pray, as John taught his disciples." And Jesus says to them when you pray say the following. And then proceeds to give the alternate Lord's Prayer.

Of course, the contents of the Lord's Prayer can change depending on which transcript you actually are reading from, but, there are some themes that run through both versions. It opens with a restoration. You reestablish your relationship with God. Father, holy is your name. May your kingdom come. Next is a reckoning. Help us to have everything we need so we don't feel the need to worry about tomorrow. We repent as we ask God to forgive our sins. We remember that even though we're not perfect God still loves us and will be with us even through those darkest moments.

So, for the Lord's prayer template you restore, reckon, repent, and remember. In the very next part of that reading Jesus assures the disciples to ask often. He assures them God's not going to get annoyed with you constantly coming up. Just like you don't get annoyed with a toddler asking mom, mom, mom, mom...eventually you turn to them and what they need, and they tell you. God wants to hear from us. God desires to be part of our life. The creator of all of this craziness and chaos down here on earth just wants to hear from you and me. It's a thought that blows my mind a little bit honestly.

The Lord's prayer Is a very solid template I'm a very solid style of prayer. If you take the time to construct your prayer based on that template, then great. But when I look at most of Jesus prayers in the Gospels the template of the Lord's prayer really seems to kind of come out of nowhere doesn't it? I mean even the prayer from today's reading doesn't follow the template of the Lord's prayer. So, what do the examples of his prayers tell us?

As with everything else the prayers from Jesus to God, that we find in scripture, show us that it's not just about the word choice, it's making sure that the words we choose when we pray sound like us. That we don't become someone different when we pray.

Our prayers to God should be authentic and personal and conversational. Just as Daniel continued to be authentic in his prayers after prayers to God were outlawed, we should find liberation in the knowledge that as spaces where it feels safe to be ourselves begin to diminish, in the presence of God will never be a space anyone can take away from us. We are expected to come to God as ourselves, unapologetically ourselves.

So, after Jesus raised Lazarus from the dead, he prayed, "Father, I thank you for having heard me. I know that you always hear me…" In Matthew he prays thank you for the time of the end of everything not being known. "I thank you, Father, Lord of Heaven and Earth, because you've hidden these things from the wise and the intelligent and have revealed them to infants." Or even the reading from today, we're a distressed and agitated and scared Jesus prayed, "Abba, Father, for you all things are possible; remove this cup from me; yet, not what I want, but, what you want."

You see these prayers are authentic to Jesus. They're personal and conversational. He's talking to God the way Adam talked to God in the garden. Our prayers should be that way also.

Our subconscious ones are. There's very little thought that goes into those. They're second nature. There's been a saying for years that as long as there is testing in schools, there will always be prayer in school. Because the subconscious prayers are always there. Those times that you mutter *"oh my god"* ...that's a prayer for help. It's a cry of exasperation. You can't believe what you're seeing.

Or how about we do one of my favorite subconscious prayers? I do this all the time when I'm feeling stressed and overwhelmed. Close your eyes, place your hands in front of you with your palms up and rest your forehead in the palm of your hands and breathe in and quickly exhale. That's a brief moment of meditation…it's a brief moment of prayer. It's an incredibly personal intimate prayer that we do all the time, but, we don't think about. Because when we get out of our way and we don't think about how we're praying to God, we just do. We do just talk to the creator.

During this time of Lent, as we work on ourselves and our relationships with each other and with God let's work on the intentionality in our prayers. That it's not just in our subconscious that we come to God, but, in our conscious state as well. Let's work on remembering that the formality in the prayers that we often hear isn't for God it's performative and is for one another. It's a personal relationship with our God. That is what God has been longing to restore with each and every one of us. That's what Easter is all about is that restoration of the relationship. And so, let's use this time of preparation to make sure that we are fully prepared to take our place in that restored relationship with God.

We Are One In The Spirit

By: Reverend Caroline Morrison
Reading: Acts 2:38-40, 44-47

Theme: Spend Time in Community

As I meditated on the idea of community for this week, I thought I'd think about the different communities that I'm a part of. You see each one of us is a collection of communities and we intersect with one another throughout those communities. Those seemingly random intersections are why the 6 degrees to Kevin Bacon game seems to work on just about everyone. I'm a member of the community of veterans...of a community of queer people, and clergy and queer veterans and queer clergy. I'm part of a community of women. I'm part of a community of liberals and of people acting in resistance to things that are happening. The number of communities that I'm a part of seems to be a list that goes on and on and on the more I think about it. And as I thought of those communities, I of course started thinking back to communities I was a part of in the past.

I really can't tell you much about where I was 10 years ago aside from saying that I was a student in seminary and the pastor of Edwardsville and Grinter Chapel United Methodist Churches in the Kansas City area. I couldn't even tell you what I was doing in March of 2015 aside from probably preaching my first Lenten series.

However, I did realize that I can tell you about March 5 years ago. Because that was March of 2020, the year that the world shut down for COVID. I can tell you that 5 years ago today, since it was a Monday, I very likely made sure the kids were started on their work and helped Zacchaeus connect to his zoom meetings and I sat at my desk with my computer and the monitors the army gave me to work from home.

I remember that we all thought it was going to be a short time. That everything was going to shut down for a little bit while people got organized, and then it just seemed to extend into oblivion. 5 years ago, this week is when all of those celebrities released the tone-deaf version of Imagine.

But there were some interesting things that happened to the community of the church because of COVID 19. The lockdowns led to a whole new level of introspection for a lot of people. People began to realize that they could worship from home. They began to realize that God wasn't sitting in a sanctuary necessarily. I mean, I could praise God on my own after all. So, the question began to be asked why did we need the church? What did the church actually provide to any of us? Why leave my home for church at all? Was there anything I got out of attending church that I didn't get from spending time with God on my own?

For many they were surprised to find that the answer was no. They got nothing more from worshiping at home than they did from going to church. They began to realize that Church had become more of a social hour in a lot of cases. So, that meant churches had to figure out what they were offering that made them different.

Now, that shouldn't have been a difficult assessment. The New Testament does have some fairly clear expectations for the home churches that are mentioned throughout Scripture. Those expectations can definitely be applied to our churches. When someone looks at our churches can they expect participation and worship? Can they expect mutual love and respect? What about moral conduct and the use of spiritual gifts? Can they anticipate unity and peace or hospitality and outreach? How about obedience to the church leadership and a focus on Christ? If those aren't things that a person can find inside the church building, then there's no reason for them to be there. Those are the things that change a fellowship into a community.

In today's reading, there wasn't just a fellowship of people. It wasn't a life that was spent with small talk and shallow personalities over a cup of lukewarm coffee and a stale cookie. The reading says that everyone who believed was together, and they had all things in common. They would sell their possessions, and their goods distribute the proceeds to all as any had need, they spent much time together in the temple and they broke bread at home and ate their food with glad and generous hearts. You could easily see God among them and that's what attracted so many people. That's why they grew the way that they did. There was a vulnerability and a reality to them that made them more real.

Those first churches practiced the 5 R's; Repent, Reckon, Remember, Restore, and Rejuvenate. Within those home churches that's what that life meant. It was almost something we would see as monastic. Within the home churches in the Acts of the Apostles, if you made a mistake or you wronged one of your siblings you repented. You went to that person, and you said I'm sorry. If you wronged the community, you repented for that as well. Paul said it was okay if anger existed don't let it rule. Be done with your anger by the end of the day so there's no space for the devil. If you're angry you **reckon** with the things that are causing the problems. You repent for your role in issues.

You remember the reason that the community exists in the first place. It exists to give everyone within it a space to grow. The community here today exists to worship God and to experience God in each other.

We **restore** our relationship with God, both, as a community, and as individuals. We work to ensure that the restoration happens so that our bonds are strengthened, and we can be strong regardless of the winds that blow to try to tear us apart.

And, finally, we are **rejuvenated** because of those around us rather than inspite of those who would rather we fall. Seeing God in those who hate us can be challenging and exhausting. But, it is necessary. So, surrounding ourselves with a community of believers that we can more easily see God within allows us to rest and recuperate in the presence of God in our siblings. We leave the presence of God rejuvenated because we've been rebuilt. We may have new ideas to think about or new revelations to contend with, but we are new creations every time we leave from the community. Regularly referencing the 5 R's as a community helps us to be as resilient and vulnerable as the home churches from which this whole faith sprung.

This table that's up here that we'll partake from a little bit later in the service, that isn't just us reliving the last supper. We partake in memory of the meals we're supposed to share with one another just like the Acts churches did. We do it in memory of Jesus and out of respect for the tradition of breaking bread with one another and the restored relationships that come from that action.

Through the breaking of bread and worship and sharing with one another, we not only experience God, we encounter God. God exists in community. Jesus said where two or more are gathered there I will be. And I remember when I was a youth thinking that it was odd that there was this weird minimum that Jesus required before he showed up. Why did there need to be two people for forgot to be present? Quite simply, it's because we encounter God in each other. I don't know if you've noticed but you can't look yourself in the eyes. Try looking at your face right now. I can see everything else, but, if I have something on my face, I need someone else to let me know. You can't gaze into the windows of your own soul. But if there are two or more gathered then you can see God in the other person, and they can see God in you. You can see God in the piece of the image of God that we each bring into the community with us.

The exercise of telling your neighbor that you see God in them isn't just something to lift spirits or lighten hearts. It's a practice that helps us to more easily see God in the people we encounter every day. In those intersecting communities that we're part of.

This setup of the sanctuary today is designed so that when you get bored looking at me, you're not just looking at the back of the head of the person seated in front of you, though I'm sure everyone here has a great looking back of your head. But it's so that each of you can look around and see God sitting among you. Do you know what happens when you see God sitting in your sanctuary with you? Everyone else starts to notice too. "As I have loved you, so you must love one another. By this everyone will know that you are my disciple, if you love one another." "They will know we are Christians by our love."

Small communities allow us to practice that love. They allow us to practice on a micro level before putting it into practice on a more macro level out in the world. Within these walls is a safe space to be vulnerable and to recharge, to let down your own walls and just let God exist around you. Beyond the walls of the church are so many obstacles to seeing God. Our own biases among those. Within these walls among this gathered group of siblings we have the opportunity to refine our display of the divine love for one another. We have the opportunity to refine our ability to see God in one another. We have the opportunity to rekindle and relight the flame within us.

But I understand, it is not easy to bring love into a world that often does not reciprocate it. Though, I'd remind you there is no asterisks on love or neighbor and there is nothing in scripture that says that those to whom we show God's love too must reflect it back. We show God's love even though there may be nothing we get back in return. The truth is that those we are called to love those that may very well continue to speak against us. They may continue to express their disdain for us. But through the love that we show them they may be able to deny our existence, but, they will not be able to deny the Spirit and Image of God that exists within us.

Because friends, Our definition of community revolves around loving God and loving one another. Our definition of community involves finding God in those we agree, and, disagree with. Our definition of community should be ever expanding beyond the walls of this church and into the many intersecting communities in which we're apart. People beyond these walls should learn to see God in each other because they're able to see God in us. Our definition of community is learning to live in peace with one another and learning to understand the way that all of our various quirks and idiosyncrasies work together to reflect God's love into the world.

The Rocks and Stones Will Sing

By Reverend Caroline Morrison
Reading: Joel 2:21-22

Theme: All of creation is God's and as stewards, we are to speak for the justice of all God's creation.

For as long as we have had stories, we have probably anthropomorphized, or given human characteristics to, the things around us. It's a practice of relatability. In 1975 the perfect pet was brought from a beach in Mexico to the shores of the United States. They sold for 4 dollars a piece and the person who discovered this pet was Gary Dahl. It was...The pet rock. People would use googly eyes and pipe cleaners to give it a personality.

Because, anthropomorphizing nature is a part of our culture. Think about the movies and books we often read; The Ents of The Lord of the Rings, Grandmother Willow from Disney's Pocahantas, the flowers from Alice in Wonderland, and Baby Groot, arguably the most adorable sapling ever, these are all examples of the plants that we have done this to in our popular culture. The idea that plants are alive while rocks are inanimate is one that is usually seen as a fact. And so, it isn't much of a stretch to then give them personalities and human understanding.

Even the Gospels have stories such as this. There is the story of Jesus cursing the fig tree on the way to the confront the money changing in the Temple. It is told in two different Gospels, Matthew and Mark. Jesus and his disciples are walking, and he is hungry. He happens upon a fig tree with no fruit and speaks to it, cursing it, causing it to shrivel up and die. Jesus also rebukes the storm and the wind, the Greek word, *epetemao,* being used in this case, is the same word used in scripture to rebuke more traditionally animate things like Satan, children, and the disciples.

The way that Jesus speaks to nature leads a person to one of two conclusions, Jesus was crazy and just spoke to everything, or, Jesus knew something about nature that we simply don't realize. The evidence of a consciousness in our environment can be found throughout scripture. "Consider the lilies of the field...they don't worry about tomorrow." Worrying is again a typically human attribute. Perhaps one of my favorite mentions is Jesus telling the Pharisees that even if the crowds were silenced, the rocks and stones would start to sing. The sound we heard at the beginning of the sermon is a prime example that this wasn't just hyperbole on the part of Jesus…NASA recorded that. It is the sound the Earth makes as it moves through space…singing as it goes. In fact, all of the bodies in the heavens produce those same recordable waves as they move through the vacuum of space. So, it becomes quite clear that the earth beneath our feet is far more than the inanimate object which we often treat it as.

In the reading today, Joel is singing a song of praise to God for all that God has done in the recent conflict. The prophet writes, "Do not fear, O soil; be glad and rejoice for the Lord has done great things!" God reassures the soil and instructs it to be glad and rejoice for the return of good fortune to the people, an escape from the misfortune and punishment that the sin of the people brought upon the land. Multiple times in Genesis we find specific stories where our actions have tremendous consequences.

In Genesis 1 we find our call to stewardship over the land. In Genesis 2 we first encounter the idea that we are simply animated soil. "Then the Lord God formed humans from the dust of the ground and breathed into his nostrils the breath of life; and the man became a living being." Our separation from the dirt beneath our feet is owed to divine CPR. Genesis 3 we find God again referencing that we are dirt, but, more importantly, it is the first time we find the liberation of the earth. See, from the beginning, we were to be stewards. Placed not just in charge, but, in partnership with the earth.

The relationship was reciprocal. We cared for the land and the plants, our siblings in creation, and in return, the land and plants would provide for us. In Genesis 3 that partnership comes crashing down and we are suddenly placed at odds with creation, Genesis 3:17b-19 states, "…cursed is the ground because of you; in toil you shall eat of it all the days of your life; thorns and thistles it shall bring forth for you; and you shall eat the plants of the field."

We find further retaliation in the story of Cain. Genesis 4:11-12a, "and now you are cursed from the ground, which has opened its mouth to receive your brother's blood from your hand. When you till the ground, it will no longer yield to you, its strength." The story of Noah and the destruction of the earth, again, is because of the sinful nature of humanity…not the sinful nature of the earth.

Perhaps that is why it is creation we hear about in so many of Jesus miracles. After all, creation didn't turn from God. Aside from that one tree, we never read about anything outside of humanity disobeying its creator. The water obeys Jesus and turns to wine. It hardens for Jesus and Peter to walk upon it. The earth shook from the innocent blood of its creator spilled upon it…and rejoiced 3 days later when the first creation was the first at the resurrection.

You see friends, the earth was also redeemed at the resurrection. Our conflict from Genesis was no longer necessary, and yet, we continue to act as if it is on-going. Our sin of misuse of water routinely leads to droughts, floods, and other disasters. Our sin of oil fracking, the practice of shooting high powered, chemical filled water between layers of earth to extract oil, has led to a rise in earthquakes in normally stable areas…such as the midwestern US. Our sin of general pollution has led to holes in the ozone layer, the extinction of species of animals and also to the rising temperatures of this planet and the global climate change. We beat the earth and through our sin, we are forced to work harder to get results from it.

There are four ecological justice areas that align with the mission of Jesus, and what should be the mission of the church, Economic, Political, Social, and Technological. Just as these were Jesus' mission, they are also our mission in all things, but, particularly in the restoring of our relationship with our sibling, creation.

So often in our ministries, we focus primarily on our relationship to each other or our relationship to God. That focus on human/human & human/divine relationships can lead to a situation where we forget our responsibility to the rest of creation. We focus on our shared problems, but, we avoid our role in the creation of those problems. Our environment, and our impact upon the environment, are often left out of our Sunday services.

So, as we look to the ecological justice areas, let us bear in mind the Rs that we find today. Let us repent of our wrongs to the earth and our fellow creation. May we reckon with the ways we have neglected our responsibility to be good stewards of these resources. And may we strive to restore our relationship with this world just as strongly as we strive to restore our relationship to God and our human siblings.

Economic

The first justice area is economic. This might not seem the most obvious, however, so much of our lives and decisions are based upon our economic situations. The food we purchase is based on our economic standing. The clothing we purchase, and the materials used to manufacture those clothes, are based on economic standing. The size of our carbon footprints is based on economic standing. As churches, we should be helping those in our communities to live lives in communion with our sibling creation, regardless of their economic standing. This can be accomplished by instituting community gardens, clothing closets stocked with natural fibers, and recycling drives, among other ideas.

The community garden means less processed food for the human system, perhaps less travel to a grocery store and less wasteful packaging for the person to dispose of at home. A community garden also returns us to a relationship with the earth more closely resembling the one outlined in the first garden in Genesis 2:15, "The Lord God took the man and put him in the Garden of Eden to till it and keep it."

A clothing closet that is stocked with natural fibers helps those in need to have clothing that is not simply comfortable, but, also more easily biodegradable. Synthetic fibers such as polyester are ultimately plastics, and, those will be around for hundreds of years. Additionally, recycling, in many communities, costs extra. Many people will forgo this to save money to spend on other essentials. Hosting regular recycling drives helps people to keep their communities clean and helps the earth.

Political

As in so many things, involvement in the political arena is part of what we are called to do as Christians. The mission and service of the church is spelled out as a social holiness emphasis by John Wesley, "Scriptural holiness entails more than personal piety; love of God, is always linked with love of neighbor, a passion for justice and renewal in the life of the world." That passion for justice applies not simply to our fellow humans, but, justice for all creation that is currently oppressed by humanity. In the political arena this typically is found in regulating and deregulating as well as the passing of laws that allow for continued waste and abuse of the land and finite resources around us.

Political environmental justice is brought about by discussing upcoming legislation and its impact upon the environment, and then of course, taking action and speaking to political representatives on behalf of our sibling creation. To provide voice for the voiceless. It's protesting, and boycotting.

Social

Social justice requires the recognition of all pieces of creation as living and helps us to not treat the earth simply as another object. A rock is inanimate, a tree is breathing, but, not human, so therefore, they can be sacrificed in favor of human interests.

Socially we must change what is acceptable about our thinking when it comes to the earth. We must pay attention to the mountains of trash that are regularly piled up. We must make waste socially unacceptable. In the grand scheme of things, a happy plate is not that important, so, don't simply clear your plate, but, only make the amount of food you will actually eat, and if you do make an abundance, feed someone else. Right now, it's socially acceptable to throw away clothing, let's change that so that the materials are reused or recycled. As an Easter people, and followers of Jesus, let us begin to change our practices. Let us find ways to reduce our energy usage, or reliance on the energy from fossil fuels and the hold they seem to have on all aspects of society.

Technological

And finally, technological justice. Like it or not, the devices that we are surrounded by will likely simply pollute the earth at some point. The battery will be thrown out, or the components of the screen will die. But, long before that happens, our individual power consumption increases. I know I have a portable charger for my devices…multiple chargers if I am being honest, and each of those chargers uses power when plugged in. Even with me at this moment is my phone, watch, and my kindle.

Think about the number of things in your home that are constantly drawing power, even when no one is around. Your television, wifi-router, alarm clocks, and with the advent of smart outlets, even when your lamps are off, the outlet can be drawing power. Even the things we do to decrease our carbon footprint can ultimately do harm. Electric vehicles, for example, use power to charge and those batteries eventually wear out and need replaced, adding further waste to our growing problems.

The technology we use can also be a major pollutant by design, Apple Computers took some hard hits in the past for the components that are used, and that isn't even discussing the lack of easily replaceable moving parts on a laptop. If one piece goes, the odds are the whole thing is toast.

While the need for Technological Environmental Justice might be easily noticeable, the fix isn't quite as obvious as the other three. The easiest solution would seem to be to unplug devices if they aren't being used, and, pay attention to how we are using them in the first place. But, let's be honest, unplugging everything in our homes and offices is not the most practical solution available. Installing the ability to shut off a wall outlet, as they have in Europe, might be a handier option.

Less obvious solutions are helping our churches to begin to implement renewable energy into renovations. Your church looking to landscape? There is a company that manufactures wind turbines that are shaped like trees. And just ensure the building is being kept up in general. I know this church has a programmable thermostat, for example, so, they aren't heating or cooling an empty building. Older buildings can leak hot and cold air from small cracks all over. Upkeep can help keep the building at least efficient if they are unable to completely cut down on their usage.

Small changes in practice and mindset are what is needed to help restore our side of our partnership with the earth. For the earth is not owned by us, we are but co-inhabitants alongside the vast ecosystem of rocks, streams, plants, predators and prey. We don't need to see our co-creation as human to empathize or sympathize, we just need to see it as marginalized. And, we need to acknowledge our role in its marginalization.

Our God speaks to the soil, rebukes the wind and water, and tells us to be more like the plants. May we find ourselves at a point that we can do just that. May we reach a point where we are partners with the earth again, able to recognize God within it, whether it is anthropomorphized and has googly eyes or not.

Off on a Hero's Journey

By Reverend Caroline Morrison
Reading: Mark 10:32-34

Theme: Walk like you don't fear where you're going.

If you have ever taken an English class, you have undoubtedly encountered the idea at some point of the hero's journey. According to Joseph Campbell, there are 12 key steps that every hero faces on their journey, and they can be categorized into 4 groups: **Departure, Trials, Transformation, and Return**. Just like with the parts of a conversation, the steps in the hero's journey are so ingrained in our cultural stories that we almost reflexively know if a part is missing or skipped. The arc feels incomplete without it.

Whether you're looking at the Lord of the Rings, or the Star Wars movies, Greek mythology, or scripture, you find those same 4 categories of the journey. Heroes such as Odysseus, Hercules, and Forrest Gump have taken part in the hero's journey. Perhaps the most interesting thing to me about the hero's journey is quite often the hero seems unaware of the epic journey they are on. The hero goes from point to point not quite realizing the grander scope that their life experiences are taking.

There's an idea that exists today as a saying among younger generations that you think you're the main character, or, that you give off main character vibes. The idea is that you act as though this story is all about you and perhaps more importantly that you don't realize the role you are playing in another person's story. The truth is that each of us is on our own hero's journey whether we recognize it or not. We are called daily to participate in transformational moments and to never stop growing in our faith, our love, and our compassion.

Our journey through lent has led us through stories of repentance, rejuvenation, remembrance, reckoning, and restoration. We recognize that we are a people for whom hiding our light is not an option. You and I are called, and created to be beacons of compassion and justice in an often unjust world. We recognize that we are a community playing a vital role in the resistance to injustice and restoration of our relationship with God. We understand that God can be seen and experienced in all people because all people are created in the image of God. And we are a people who seek justice not just for ourselves, not just for our community, but for all of creation...because the resurrection wasn't just for humans, it was a victory for all of creation.

Our hero's journey is one of liberation. It's a journey of redemption and one of restoration. Within the next weeks we celebrate the resurrection of Jesus. Within the next weeks we will recall the events taking place that Jesus spoke of in the reading today, and, our hero's journey comes face to face with the question of whether we once again are willing to face our fears head on and go forward, or, are we so exhausted that we long to quit and allow ourselves to stagnate?

Because, as resilient as we wish to be, we are a community of humans, and we are fatigued to say the least. We are battered, we are bruised, and we are exhausted. And it is OK to acknowledge that. There is nothing in the hero's journey that says the hero can't acknowledge the reality of their situation. There is nothing in the hero's journey that says we can't feel hopeless or in despair. There is nothing prohibiting the hero from dwelling in depression and self-doubt. Honestly, that moment when all seems lost is almost a pre-requisite. It must be dark before the dawn in the hero's journey.

In fact, in the reading today, Jesus is trying to get his disciples to see exactly that. That the days to come are going to get quite dark. Jesus paraphrases beautifully for his disciples in the reading the reality of what is about to take place. He says, we're going to Jerusalem, I'm going to be handed over to the chief priests and scribes and condemned to death. They'll hand me to the gentiles, and I'll be tortured and beaten and killed, and then three days later I'll rise again.

Now Jesus detaches himself some by speaking in the third person, essentially. The red-letter quote is talking about the son of man. But we know he's talking about himself. Still, the important thing is that he knows what is to take place. He knows what is to come. He knows he is about to have an amazing moment in his ministry with the triumphant entry into Jerusalem, before everything falls apart. And yet, knowing what's to come he continues on despite his fear.

Examples of that kind of perseverance in the face of a fear that would otherwise be debilitating permeate throughout scripture. In the book of Esther, she outs herself to the king and confronts him about his order against the Jews. Moses returns to Egypt after murdering an Egyptian to confront his brother who now sits on the throne. David and Goliath. The Syrophoenician woman, and the woman at the well. And, of course, Jeremiah for whom God specifically says, "... For you shall go to all to whom I send you, and you shall speak whatever I command you. Do not be afraid of them, for I am with you to deliver you..." Or, Psalm 23, "Even though I walk through the darkest valley, I fear no evil; for you are with me; your rod and your staff---they comfort me." Those scriptural stories lend credence to the notion that we are not alone in our fights and that we are supported, and empowered, in our fights against injustice.

It is also powerful to see that those stories exist in within non-biblical context as well. People like Dietrich Bonhoeffer wrote and spoke against the Third Reich. He even opened his own theological school in an effort to continue to educate future generations on true Christianity versus the fascist version that had started to be popularized. Herr Bonhoffer stood at a time when his friends and colleagues crumbled. And he met his end for it. He wound up being sent first to Auschwitz and then to a different concentration camp where he eventually was executed. He never once denied the reality of the situation he was responding to. He never denied the fear he felt of the repercussions that he would likely face. He simply knew that he had a bigger job to do than fear would allow.

But the message from this is not that you shouldn't feel fear. The message is not that fear shouldn't have an impact on your life. The fact is that the feeling of fear is human. We've talked about that before. The feeling of fear and of dread towards a future that you know will be hard is a natural part of being human. But it is not the only part.

We are empowered by God to move beyond that fear. We are empowered by God to speak through our fear. To act through our fear. We are empowered by God to unashamedly shine in spite of our fear. To be Christian is to know that we are called to more than fear. Christianity is not simply of religion. Christian is not simply an adjective describing a noun. Christian is a series of verbs.

When someone finds out that I am a Christian, I want them to immediately assume that I am politically progressive. When someone finds out that I'm a Christian, I want them to immediately assume that I sit on the side of truth and justice. When someone finds out I'm a Christian, I want them to immediately assume that I do not condone idolatry, that I do not condone greed, that I do not condone the powerful acting only within their own self-interest, and I want anyone who finds out that I'm a Christian to know that, just as Jesus did before me, I will stand and march beside anyone without the privilege I have, and I will amplify the voice of any of my siblings who are silenced from the margins.

"They will know we are Christians by our love…" does not mean that we are simply peaceful, passive, pacifists. We are not called to be solely submissive to the state. You and I are called to be thorns in the side of those who are unjust. We are to be pebbles in the shoes of those who would walk all over us. When our siblings who share the margins with us are stomped down, we are called to rise and lift them with us.

Now, I would be lying if I told you that I was unafraid of what is to come. I would be lying if I told you that I was unafraid of the backlash to the growing crowds and the increasing volume of the critical voices of what's happening in the government. I've seen too many dystopian futures written about in books and shown on screen to not feel fear of an inevitable crackdown on using my voice. But being Christian is knowing that God is bigger than the fear I feel. Allowing myself to be filled with the spirit means allowing the spirit to move my feet, and, part my lips, and, give me the words.

So, as lent comes to an end, may we exit just as Jesus exited the desert, prepared to unapologetically conduct our ministry. When we are told to be silent or to quiet down, may we be like the rocks and stones and continue to sing. May our resistance and resilience make us thistles and dandelions in the garden of evil that our leaders seem desperate to grow. And as we face the path of darkness that looms before us, may we always remember we are bearers of the image and light of God, the creator of all existence, and that we do not walk that dark path alone, for our siblings in Christ and our almighty God travel with us.

Made in the USA
Monee, IL
25 April 2025

16336424R10075